Books by Steven D. Price

The Horseman's Illustrated Dictionary
Essential Riding
The Quotable Horse Lover
The Kids' Book of the American Quarter Horse
The American Quarter Horse: An Introduction to Selection, Care, and Enjoyment
Caught Me a Big 'Un
(with Jimmy Houston)
The Ultimate Fishing Guide
The Polo Primer
(with Charles Kauffman)
Riding for a Fall
All the King's Horses: The Story of the Budweiser Clydesdales
Riding's a Joy
(with Joy Slater)
The Whole Horse Catalog
(with Barbara Burn, Gail Rentsch, Werner Rentsch, and David A. Spector)
Schooling to Show: Basics of Hunter-Jumper Training
(with Antonio D'Ambrosio Jr.)
Horseback Vacation Guide
Old as the Hills: The Story of Bluegrass Music
The Second-Time Single Man's Survival Handbook
(with William J. Gordon)
Take Me Home: The Rise of Country-and-Western Music
Get a Horse! Basics of Backyard Horsekeeping
Panorama of American Horses
Teaching Riding at Summer Camp

The
Greatest
Horse Stories
Ever Told

EDITED AND WITH AN INTRODUCTION BY
STEVEN D. PRICE

THE LYONS PRESS
Guilford, Connecticut
An imprint of The Globe Pequot Press

The Globe Pequot Press, P. O. Box 480, Guilford, CT 06437.

The Lyons Press is an imprint of The Globe Pequot Press.

Printed in the United States of America

10 9 8 7 6 5 4 3 2 1

Design by Compset, Inc.

The Library of Congress Cataloging-in-Publication Data is available on file.

Contents

General Introduction

Reading an anthology of short fiction, essays and articles about horses may be an entertainment, but compiling one is a real education.

As someone who has spent literally the better part of his life delving into equestrian literature, and doing so with the interest and enthusiasm that approach that of being around horses, I had no reluctance to take on the task. A plethora of writing was out there, I knew. However, what I hadn't realized was the number of selections from which to draw. The easy part of the job was locating and then reading the candidates; making the choices was the hard part.

In the course of compiling this volume, I discovered that a disproportionate number of candidates, both fiction and nonfiction, dealt with thoroughbred racing and foxhunting. The reason would at first blush appear to have to do with the British sporting tradition, since both pursuits trace their origins to the British Isles.

However, success in racing and hunting also involves huge amounts of uncertainty—some would call it luck—which is the stuff of which high drama and low comedy and every other kind of literature in between are made.

By the same token, I was surprised by the rarity of good writing about another sport with British connections, polo. Although Kipling's "The Maltese Cat" is a notable exception, that story appears in so many other equestrian anthologies that to omit it here was an easy decision to make. Perhaps sometime soon writers will rectify the lack of good polo stories; the sport certainly provides ample fodder.

The selections reveal a wide range of activities in which horses take part. That was entirely intentional. In addition to racing and hunting are dressage, cutting, draft horses, western ranch work, show jumping, driving, and several aspects of pleasure riding and of training the horse and rider. It was also my intention that readers who are involved in one of these disciplines or perhaps in one that has not been included will find something of value in all the selections.

The variety of styles and purposes will help in that regard. You will find humor in the selections by Cooky McClung and Damon Runyon, inspiration in the ones by Gene Smith and Ellie Phayer, nostalgia in Clarence Day and Ben Green, instructiveness in Tom McGuane and Colonel Podhajsky, lyricism in Felix Salten and James Herriott, and pure emotion in Esther Forbes and William Nack. Indeed, something for everyone.

Despite the diversity of subject matter and style, there is, I would suggest, a certain commonality. Joseph Conrad saw the writer's task as "by the power of the written word, to make you hear, to make you feel—that is, before all, to make you see." By sharing their experiences with and insights into horses, all the authors allow us take part in competitive victories and losses, training advances and frustrations, companionship, exhilaration and sadness, self-realizations, life and death. Through the perceptions and narrative power of these writers, we are able to view and, in no small way, to understand horses just as clearly as we see them in works by Stubbs, Remington, Munnings or any other great sporting artist.

And, as if looking into a mirror held up to life, we come to see not only horses but ourselves in relation to the animal we prize above all others.

—Steven D. Price

The
Greatest
Horse Stories
Ever Told

Mr. T.'s Heart

BY JANE SMILEY

Jane Smiley, who won the 1992 Pulitzer Prize for fiction for *A Thousand Acres,* is an accomplished equestrienne. Articles on a variety of subjects involving horses and riding, such as this one, have appeared in *Practical Horseman* and other magazines.

I always suspected Mr. T. had one of those large economy-size thoroughbred hearts: maybe not Secretariat size (twenty-two pounds) or Mill Reef size (seventeen pounds), but larger and stronger than average (seven pounds). The horse was a fitness machine.

In five years of riding and eventing, I had never tired him out. He was always ready for more, even if I was nearly falling off him from the exertion.

Every year at his well-horse checkup, the vet would comment on his dropped beats—he could drop two or even three (five seconds between two heartbeats seems like a very long time when the horse is standing before you, apparently alive and well)—and attribute it to the residual effect of a great deal of exercise early in life. (He was a racehorse for eight years and had fifty-two starts.) Thus it was that I wasn't too worried when this year, Mr. T.'s twenty-first, the vet detected what he called arrhythmia. As I was taking another horse up to the vet clinic at UC Davis anyway, I packed Mr. T. along.

The results weren't good. On the one hand, the senior cardiologist shook my hand and thanked me for bringing him a big, lean thoroughbred with a heart that was so efficient and powerful that through the stethoscope it was nearly deafening. On the other hand, that arrhythmia had a name. It was "atrial fibrillation"; and it wasn't just a quirk, it was a potentially dangerous condition. The horse could drop dead at any moment.

I was impressed in spite of myself (and in spite of my conviction that Mr. T. was going to live forever) and agreed to have him "converted"—that is, to allow the cardiologist to administer a powerful and toxic drug, quinidine, that might or might not convert his chaotic heart rhythm to a normal or "sinous" rhythm. It was an in-patient procedure. I left him there and brought my other horse home.

Mr. T. was a very bad patient. He wouldn't eat, wouldn't relax, would hardly drink. His separation anxiety was so great that the cardiologist actually feared for his survival. He did, however, "convert"—his heart rhythm returned to normal, without any dropped beats—and stayed converted.

The bad news was that the dose it had taken to convert him was very close to toxic. There would be no trying this again. And the quinidine took maybe twice as long to clear his system as usual, putting him at risk in other ways.

I tried not to pay attention to the cardiologist's other remark—that the longer the heart had been arrhythmic, the less likely a permanent conversion. Those dropped beats we had always heard—I wasn't going to admit the possibility that his heart had been arrhythmic as long as I had known him.

As some readers of this magazine may know, Mr. T. (profiled in November 1998's "Why I Can't Find a New Horse") had stopped being a jumper—age, an eye injury, and timidity on my part. But not long after I wrote about him, he started jumping again, and he was great at it, as he had once been—energetic, fast, and full of thrust. And there was no changing his go-for-it style. I'd tried that, and it had just made him confused and anxious. You couldn't parse a fence or a combination or a course and try to get him to jump in a relaxed, easy style. You had to sit up, hold on, and let him do it. It was hugely exciting.

Anyway, two weeks after the conversion, Mike, my local vet, took another EKG. Tick Tock Tick Tock (that was the horse's real name), everything was perfect. I began conditioning Mr. T. for an event at the end of June.

I was well organized in my training, for once. I had him entered in a schooling show, in a couple of jumper classes, and I was galloping him at a local training track once a week. At the beginning of June, I took him over to the track, a half-mile oval. As soon as we entered the gate, he picked up a huge, even, ground-covering trot on very light contact. He trotted happily, his ears pricked, for two miles. Then I walked him half a mile and asked for the canter. For a mile, it was collected, even, easy, a perfect joy. Then I walked him again.

At the last, I gave in to impulse. After he had caught his breath, I turned him, bridged my reins, and assumed galloping position. I said, out loud,

"Pick your own pace," and he did. He took hold and shot forward, switching leads and going faster about every eighth of a mile, exactly like a racehorse. But then, he was always a racehorse. The other stuff was just for fun.

For me, the "breeze" was both frightening and exhilarating—as fast as I had ever gone on a horse, but incredibly stable. Yes, I was not in control, but he was, and I never doubted that he knew exactly where each foot was at every stride. More important, all this exercise was effortless. He was hardly blowing after we had gone half a mile and I managed to bring him down. It took him the usual ten minutes to cool out.

Three days later, we went to the show. He warmed up and jumped around perfectly, won a couple of ribbons, seemed happy.

Thus it was that I couldn't believe it, four days after that, when Mike told me that his atrial fibrillation was back, and possibly worse. His heart rhythm was chaotic. We took another EKG, sent it off to Davis, discussed it more than necessary with lots of vets. The cardiologist's recommendation was discouraging—walking around, maybe a little trotting from time to time. But, I said. But. But when I galloped him on the track, the work was effortless for him.

The answer to the riddle was in his large, strong heart. He had enough overcapacity to give himself some leeway, to oxygenate himself thoroughly almost all of the time. The danger, to me as well as to him, was that his overcapacity was unpredictable. He could literally be doing fine one moment and drop dead the next. And, the cardiologist suggested, in accordance with the no-free-lunch principle, greater-than-average heart size often went with arrhythmia. His recommendation stayed the same—walking, a little jogging from time to time.

I stopped riding the horse. I'm not sure why, except that I was confused and ambivalent. One day I decided to ignore the cardiologist's advice, the next day I decided to heed it. Mr. T. and I were used to working, and working pretty hard. If we weren't allowed to work hard together, then what? I didn't know. I let him hang out in the pasture with his broodmare friend.

Not too long ago, I decided to pretty much ignore the cardiologist. I wouldn't be stupid and run Mr. T. cross-country or "breeze" him again, but I would do dressage and jump and treat him like a normal horse.

That very day, I went out to give him a carrot, and he was standing in the shade, pawing the ground. I put him in a stall with lots of water and no food—he'd been colicky before. By bedtime, he had manured three or four times.

In the morning he seemed right as rain, so I began introducing a bit of hay. He continued to seem fine. After noon, I let him out. An hour later, he was pawing and looking at his flanks. I called Mike, who was engaged but promised to come ASAP.

Half an hour later, the horse was eating manure. My heart sank. Even though Mike and another vet I asked said this meant nothing with regard to colic, I knew differently. I had never seen him do such a thing, and I thought it was an act of equine desperation.

The rest of the day was a losing battle. No matter how much painkiller of whatever kind we gave him, the pain could not be alleviated. And his atrial fibrillation meant that he could not tolerate surgery. The impaction, which may or may not have been a torsion, was out of reach and would not dissolve. At 10:00 P.M., I said to Mike, "Are you telling me now's the time?"

He said, "Yes."

I led Mr. T. out of the lighted stall where we had been trying to treat him. He moved, but his head was down and he was hardly conscious of me. We went out into the grassy pasture where he had wandered at large every day of the spring. I knelt down in front of my horse's lowered head, and I told him what a wonderful horse he was, perfect from top to toe every minute. Then Mike gave him the two big shots of barbiturates that would cause him to arrest.

Arrest what?

His heart.

It didn't take more than a second or two. Mike held the lead rope. The collapse of a horse is always earth-shaking. His haunches drop backward, his head flies up, his knees buckle, he fells to the side. We flocked around him, petting and talking to him, but he was gone already.

After everyone left, my boyfriend and I covered him with blankets and went in the house.

I slept fitfully, unable to grasp the suddenness and enormity of the death of my dear friend and constant companion. Each time I woke up, I dreaded going out there at daybreak—what would he look like? How would the mare be acting? What would I do next with a thirteen-hundred-pound body?

When it was finally time to get up, my boyfriend got up with me, and we went out. The mare was in her stall, quiet. I fed her. Then we approached the mound. Fermentation from the impacted food had already begun—under the blanket, my horse's belly was beginning visibly to swell.

I folded back the cover, expecting something horrible, but Mr. T.'s eyes were closed—a kindness my boyfriend had done me the night before. I can't express how important this was. It was not that I had ever seen his eyes closed before. I had not—he was too alert to sleep in my presence. Rather, it was that, looking familiarly asleep, he looked uniquely at peace.

We sat down next to his head and stroked and petted him and talked. I admired, once again, his well-shaped ears, his beautiful head and throatlatch, his open nostrils, his silky coat, his textbook front legs that raced fifty-two times, in addition to every other sort of equine athletic activity, and were as clean at twenty years old as the day he was born. I admired his big, round, hard feet.

But we didn't just talk to him and about him. We relaxed next to him, stroking and petting, and talking about other things, too. We felt the coolness of his flesh, and it was pleasant, not gruesome. We stayed with him long enough to recognize that he was not there, that this body was like a car he had driven and now had gotten out of. The mare watched us, but she, too, was calm.

Later, when I spoke to the manager of my other mares and foals, she told me that when a foal dies, you always leave it with the mare for a while—long enough for her to realize fully that it is not going to get up again, and to come to terms with that. I thought then that this is true of people, too. We have to experience the absence of life in order to accept it.

My friends know that I adored Mr. T. to a boring and sometimes embarrassing degree. I would *kvell* at the drop of a riding helmet about his every quirk and personal quality. He was a good, sturdy, handsome horse, and a stakes winner, but not a horse of unusual accomplishment or exceptional beauty. He was never unkind and never unwilling—those were his special qualities. Nevertheless, I watched him and doted over him and appreciated him day after day for almost six years.

The result is a surprising one. I miss him less, rather than more. Having loved him in detail (for example, the feel of his right hind leg stepping under me, then his left hind, then his right hind again . . . for example, the sight of his ears pricking as he caught sight of me over his stall door . . . for example, the sight of him strolling across his paddock . . . for example, the feel in my hands of him taking hold and coming under as we approached a fence . . . for example, the sound of his nicker), I have thousands of clear images of him right with me. I think I miss him less than I thought I would because I don't feel him to be absent.

There is no way to tell non-horsey people that the companionship of a horse is not like that of a dog, or a cat, or a person. Perhaps the closest two consciousnesses can ever come is the wordless simultaneity of horse and rider focusing together on a jump or a finish line or a canter pirouette, and then executing what they have intended together. What two bodies are in such continuous, prolonged closeness as those of a horse and rider completing a hundred-mile endurance ride or a three-day event? I have a friend who characterizes riding as "one nervous system taking over another." I often wonder—which is doing the taking over, and which is being taken over?

I never expected to be writing this article. Rather, I intended, in twenty years, to write, "Oldest Known Equine Is Seventeen-Hand Ex-Racehorse." But I see it is time to take my own advice, the advice I gave my daughter when she got her first real boyfriend. I told her that no matter what happened with this boyfriend, once she had experienced the joys of a happy and close relationship, she would always know how to have that again, and would always have that again. And the truth is, that works for horses, too.

The Lady Who Rides to Hounds

From *Hunting Sketches*

BY ANTHONY TROLLOPE

The nineteenth-century British author Anthony Trollope, best known for his Barchester novels, was a passionate horseman. For example, whenever he traveled around Ireland in his capacity of postal inspector, he rode one horse and led another; when he encountered a foxhunt in progress, he tied his hack to a tree and set off on his hunter to join in. At the end of the hunt, he simply changed mounts and continued about his business.

This selection provides a droll analysis of foxhunting and the men and women who ride to hounds.

Among those who hunt there are two classes of hunting people who always like it, and these people are hunting parsons and hunting ladies. That it should be so is natural enough. In the life and habits of parsons and ladies there is much that is antagonistic to hunting, and they who suppress this antagonism do so because they are Nimrods at heart. But the riding of these horsemen under difficulties—horsemen and horsewomen—leaves a strong impression on the casual observer of hunting; for to such an one it seems that the hardest riding is forthcoming exactly where no hard riding should be expected. On the present occasion I will, if you please, confine myself to the lady who rides to hounds, and will begin with an assertion, which will not be contradicted, that the number of such ladies is very much on the increase.

Women who ride, as a rule, ride better than men. They, the women, have always been instructed; whereas men have usually come to ride without any instruction. They are put upon ponies when they are all boys, and put themselves upon their fathers' horses as they become hobbledehoys: and thus they obtain the power of sticking on to the animal while he gallops and jumps—and even while he kicks and shies; and, so progressing, they achieve an amount of horsemanship which answers the purposes of life. But they do not acquire the art of riding with exactness, as women do, and rarely have such hands as a woman has on a horse's mouth. The consequence of this is that women fall less often than men, and the field is not often thrown into the horror which would arise were a lady known to be in a ditch with a horse lying on her.

I own that I like to see three or four ladies out in a field, and I like it the better if I am happy enough to count one or more of them among my own acquaintances. Their presence tends to take off from hunting that character of horseyness—of both fast horseyness and slow horseyness—which has become, not unnaturally, attached to it, and to bring it within the category of gentle sports. There used to prevail an idea that the hunting man was of necessity loud and rough, given to strong drinks, ill adapted for the poetries of life, and perhaps a little prone to make money out of his softer friend. It may now be said that this idea is going out of vogue, and that hunting men are supposed to have that same feeling with regard to their horses—the same and no more—which ladies have for their carriage or soldiers for their swords. Horses are valued simply for the services that they can render, and are only valued highly when they are known to be good servants. That a man may hunt without drinking or swearing, and may possess a nag or two without any propensity to sell it or them for double their value, is now beginning to be understood. The oftener that women are to be seen "out," the more will such improved feelings prevail as to hunting, and the pleasanter will be the field to men who are not horsey, but who may nevertheless be good horsemen. There are two classes of women who ride to hounds, or rather, among many possible classifications, there are two to which I will now call attention. There is the lady who rides, and demands assistance; and there is the lady who rides, and demands none. Each always—I may say always—receives all the assistance that she may require; but the difference between the two, to the men who ride with them, is very great. It will, of course, be understood that, as to both these samples of female Nimrods, I speak of ladies who really ride—not of those who grace the coverts with, and disappear under the auspices of, their papas or their grooms when the work begins.

The lady who rides and demands assistance in truth becomes a nuisance before the run is over, let her beauty be ever so transcendent, her horsemanship ever-so perfect, and her battery of general feminine artillery ever so powerful. She is like the American woman, who is always wanting your place in a railway carriage—and demanding it, too, without the slightest idea of paying you for it with thanks; whose study it is to treat you as though she ignored your existence while she is appropriating your services. The hunting lady who demands assistance is very particular about her gates, requiring that aid shall be given to her with instant speed, but that the man who gives it shall never allow himself to be hurried as he renders it. And she soon becomes reproachful—oh, so soon! It is marvellous to watch the manner in which a hunting lady will become exacting, troublesome, and at last imperious—deceived and spoilt by the attention which she receives. She teaches herself to think at last that a man is a brute who does not ride as though he were riding as her servant, and that it becomes her to assume indignation if every motion around her is not made with some reference to her safety, to her comfort, or to her success. I have seen women look as Furies look, and heard them speak as Furies are supposed to speak, because men before them could not bury themselves and their horses out of their way at a moment's notice, or because some pulling animal would still assert himself while they were there, and not sink into submission and dog-like obedience for their behoof.

I have now before my eyes one who was pretty, brave, and a good horse-woman; but how men did hate her! When you were in a line with her there was no shaking her off. Indeed, you were like enough to be shaken off yourself, and to be rid of her after that fashion. But while you were with her you never escaped her at a single fence, and always felt that you were held to be trespassing against her in some manner. I shall never forget her voice—"Pray, take care of that gate." And yet it was a pretty voice, and elsewhere she was not given to domineering more than is common to pretty women in general; but she had been taught badly from the beginning, and she was a pest. It was the same at every gap. "Might I ask you not to come too near me?" And yet it was impossible to escape her. Men could not ride wide of her, for she would not ride wide of them. She had always some male escort with her, who did not ride as she rode, and consequently, as she chose to have the advantage of an escort—of various escorts—she was always in the company of some who did not feel as much joy in the presence of a pretty young woman as men should do under all circumstances. "Might I ask you not to come too near me?" If she could only have heard the remarks to which this constant little request of hers gave rise. She is now the mother of children, and her hunting days are gone, and probably she never makes that little request. Doubtless that look, made up partly of offence and partly of female dignity, no longer clouds her brow. But I fancy that they who knew her of old in the hunting field never approach her now without fancying that they hear those reproachful words, and see that powerful look of injured feminine weakness.

But there is the hunting lady who rides hard and never asks for assistance. Perhaps I may be allowed to explain to embryo Dianas—to the growing huntresses of the present age—that she who rides and makes no demand receives attention as close as it ever given to her more imperious sister. And how welcome she is! What a grace she lends to the day's sport! How pleasant it is to see her in her pride of place, achieving her mastery over the difficulties in her way by her own wit—as all men, and all women also, must really do who intend to ride to hounds; and doing it all without any sign that the difficulties are too great for her!

The lady who rides like this is in truth seldom in the way. I have heard men declare that they would never wish to see a side-saddle in the field because women are troublesome, and because they must be treated with attention lest the press of the moment be ever so instant. From this I dissent altogether. The small amount of courtesy that is needed is more than atoned for by the grace of her presence, and in fact produces no more impediment in the hunting-field than in other scenes of life. But in the hunting-field, as in other scenes, let assistance never be demanded by a woman. If the lady finds that she cannot keep a place in the first flight without such demands on the patience of those around her, let her acknowledge to herself that the attempt is not in her line, and that it should be abandoned. If it be the ambition of a hunting lady to ride straight—and women have very much of this ambition—let her use her eyes but never her voice; and let her ever have a smile for those who help her in her little difficulties. Let her never ask any one "to take care of that gate," or look as though she expected the profane crowd to keep aloof from her. So shall she win the hearts of those around her, and go safely through brake and brier, over ditch and dyke, and meet with a score of knights around her who will be willing and able to give her eager aid should the chance of any moment require it.

There are two accusations which the more demure portion of the world is apt to advance against hunting ladies—or, as I should better say, against hunting as an amusement for ladies. It leads to flirting, they say—to flirting of a sort which mothers would not approve; and it leads to fast habits—to ways and thoughts which are of the horse horsey—and of the stable, strongly tinged with the rack and manger. The first of these accusations is, I think, simply made in ignorance. As girls are brought up among us now-a-days, they may all flirt, if they have a mind to do so; and opportunities for flirting are much better and much more commodious in the ball-room, in the drawing-room, or in the park, than they are in the hunting-field. Nor is the work in hand of a nature to create flirting tendencies—as, it must be admitted, is the nature of the work in hand when the floors are waxed and the fiddles are going. And this error has sprung from, or forms part of, another, which is wonderfully common among non-hunting folk. It is very widely thought by many, who do not, as a rule, put themselves in opposition to the amusements of the world, that hunting in itself is a wicked thing; that hunting men are fast, given to unclean living and bad ways of life; that they usually go to bed drunk, and that they go about the world roaring hunting cries, and disturbing the peace of the innocent generally. With such men, who could wish that wife, sister, or daughter should associate? But I venture to say that this opinion, which I believe to be common, is erroneous, and that men who hunt are not more iniquitous than men who go out fishing, or play dominoes, or dig in their gardens. Maxima debetur pueris reverentia, and still more to damsels; but if boys and girls will never go where they will hear more to injure them than they will usually do amidst the ordinary conversation of a hunting field, the maxima reverentia will have been attained.

As to that other charge, let it be at once admitted that the young lady who has become of the horse horsey has made a fearful, almost a fatal mistake. And so also has the young man who falls into the same error. I hardly know to which such phase of character may be most injurious. It is a pernicious vice, that of succumbing to the beast that carries you, and making yourself, as it were, his servant, instead of keeping him ever as yours. I will not deny that I have known a lady to fall into this vice from hunting; but so also have I known ladies to marry their music-masters and to fall in love with their footmen. But not on that account are we to have no music-masters and no footmen.

Let the hunting lady, however, avoid any touch of this blemish, remembering that no man ever likes a woman to know as much about a horse as he thinks he knows himself.

Pure Heart

BY WILLIAM NACK

I had the unusual opportunity to watch Secretariat's Belmont States triumph on the television set in the jockey's room at Hollywood Park race track. When the horse cantered home by 32 lengths, everyone in the room—and those jocks, valets and others were as unsentimental a group of veteran hardboots as ever gathered under one roof—stood up and applauded.

Published in *Sports Illustrated,* William Nack's tribute to Secretariat movingly captures the universal appeal of that great horse.

Just before noon the horse was led haltingly into a van next to the stallion barn, and there a concentrated barbiturate was injected into his jugular. Forty-five seconds later there was a crash as the stallion collapsed. His body was trucked immediately to Lexington, Ky., where Dr. Thomas Swerczek, a professor of veterinary science at the University of Kentucky, performed the necropsy. All of the horse's vital organs were normal in size except for the heart.

"We were all shocked," Swerczek said. "I've seen and done thousands of autopsies on horses, and nothing I'd ever seen compared to it. The heart of the average horse weighs about nine pounds. This was almost twice the average size, and a third larger than any equine heart I'd ever seen. And it wasn't pathologically enlarged. All the chambers and the valves were normal. It was just larger. I think it told us why he was able to do what he did."

In the late afternoon of Monday, Oct. 2, 1989, as I headed my car from the driveway of Arthur Hancock's Stone Farm onto Winchester Road outside Paris, Ky., I was seized by an impulse as beckoning as the wind that strums through the trees down there, mingling the scents of new grass and old history.

For reasons as obscure to me then as now, I felt compelled to see Lawrence Robinson. For almost 30 years, until he suffered a stroke in March 1983, Robinson was the head caretaker of stallions at Claiborne Farm. I had not seen him since his illness, but I knew he still lived on the farm, in a small white frame house set on a hill overlooking the lush stallion paddocks and the main stallion barn. In the first stall of that barn, in the same place that was once home to the great Bold Ruler, lived Secretariat, Bold Ruler's greatest son.

It was through Secretariat that I had met Robinson. On the bright, cold afternoon of Nov. 12, 1973, Robinson was one of several hundred people gathered at Blue Grass Airport in Lexington to greet Secretariat after his flight from New York into retirement in Kentucky. I flew with the horse that day, and as the plane banked over the field, a voice from the tower crackled over the airplane radio: "There's more people out here to meet Secretariat than there was to greet the governor."

"Well, he's won more races than the governor," pilot Dan Neff replied.

An hour later, after a ran ride out the Paris Pike behind a police escort with blue lights flashing, Robinson led Secretariat onto a ramp at Claiborne and toward his sire's old stall—out of racing and into history. For me, that final walk beneath a grove of trees, with the colt slanting like a buck through the autumn gloaming, brought to a melancholy close the richest, grandest, damnedest, most exhilarating time of my life. For eight months, first as the racing writer for *Newsday* of Long Island, N.Y., and then as the designated chronicler of Secretariat's career, I had a daily front-row seat to watch the colt. I was at the barn in the morning and the racetrack in the afternoon for what turned out to be the year's greatest show in sports, at the heart of which lay a Triple Crown performance unmatched in the history of American racing.

Sixteen years had come and gone since then, and I had never attended a Kentucky Derby or a yearling sale at Keeneland without driving out to Claiborne to visit Secretariat, often in the company of friends who had never seen him. On the long ride from Louisville, I would regale my friends with stories about the horse—how on that early morning in March '73 he had materialized out of the quickening blue darkness in the upper stretch at Belmont Park, his ears pinned back, running as fast as horses run; how he had lost the Wood Memorial and won the Derby, and how he had been bothered by a pigeon feather at Pimlico on the eve of the Preakness (at the end of this tale I would pluck the delicate, mashed feather out of my wallet, like a picture of my kids, to pass around the car); how on the morning of the Belmont Stakes he had burst from the barn like a stud horse going to the breeding shed and had walked around the outdoor ring on his hind legs, pawing at the sky; how he had once grabbed my notebook and refused to give it back, and how he had seized a rake in his teeth and begun raking the shed; and, finally, I told about that magical, unforgettable instant, frozen now in time, when he turned for home, appearing out of a dark drizzle at Woodbine, near Toronto, in the last race of his career, 12 lengths in front and steam puffing from his nostrils as from a factory whistle, bounding like some mythical beast of Greek lore.

Oh, I knew all the stories, knew them well, had crushed and rolled them in my hand until their quaint musk lay in the saddle of my palm. Knew them as I knew the stories of my children. Knew them as I knew the stories of my own life. Told them at dinner parties, swapped them with horseplayers as if they were trading cards, argued over them with old men and blind fools who had seen the show but missed the message. Dreamed them and turned them over like pillows in my rubbery sleep. Woke up with them, brushed my aging teeth with them, grinned at them in the mirror. Horses have a way of getting inside you, and so it was that Secretariat became like a fifth child in our house, the older boy who was off at school and never around but who was as loved and true a part of the family as Muffin, our shaggy, epileptic dog.

The story I now tell begins on that Monday afternoon last October on the macadam outside Stone Farm. I had never been to Paris, Ky., in the early fall, and I only happened to be there that day to begin an article about the Hancock family, the owners of Claiborne and Stone farms. There wasn't a soul on the road to point the way to Robinson's place, so I swung in and out of several empty driveways until I saw a man on a tractor cutting the lawn in front of Marchmont, Dell Hancock's mansion. He yelled back to me: "Take a right out the drive. Go down to Claiborne House. Then a right at the driveway across that road. Go up a hill to the big black barn. Turn left and go down to the end. Lawrence had a stroke a few years back, y'know."

The house was right where he said. I knocked on the front door, then walked behind and knocked on the back and called through a side window into a room where music was playing. No one answered. But I had time to kill, so I wandered over to the stallion paddock, just a few yards from the house. The stud Ogygian, a son of Damascus, lifted his head inquiringly. He started walking toward me, and I put my elbows on the top of the fence and looked down the gentle slope toward the stallion barn.

And suddenly there he was, Secretariat, standing outside the barn and grazing at the end of a lead shank held by groom Bobby Anderson, who was sitting on a bucket in the sun. Even from a hundred yards away, the horse appeared lighter than I had seen him in years. It struck me as curious that he was not running free in his paddock—why was Bobby grazing him?—but his bronze coat reflected the October light, and it never occurred to me that something might be wrong. But something was terribly wrong. On Labor Day, Secretariat had come down with laminitis, a life-threatening hoof disease, and here, a month later, he was still suffering from its aftershocks.

Secretariat was dying. In fact, he would be gone within 48 hours.

I briefly considered slipping around Ogygian's paddock and dropping down to visit, but I had never entered Claiborne through the backdoor, so I thought better of it. Instead, for a full half hour, I stood by the paddock waiting for Robinson and gazing at Secretariat. The gift of reverie is a blessing divine, and it is conferred most abundantly on those who lie in hammocks or drive alone in cars. Or lean on hillside fences in Kentucky. The mind swims, binding itself to whatever flotsam comes along, to old driftwood faces and voices of the past, to places and scenes once visited, to things not seen or done but only dreamed.

It was July 4, 1972, and I was sitting in the press box at Aqueduct with Clem Florio, a former prizefighter turned Baltimore handicapper, when I glanced at the *Daily Racing Form*'s past performances for the second race, a 5½-furlong buzz for maiden 2-year-olds. As I scanned the pedigrees, three names leaped out: by Bold Ruler–Somethingroyal, by Princequillo. Bold Ruler was the nation's preeminent sire, and Somethingroyal was the dam of several stakes winners, including the fleet Sir Gaylord. It was a match of royalty. Even the baby's name seemed faintly familiar: Secretariat. Where had I heard it before? But of course! Lucien Laurin was training the colt at Belmont Park for Penny Chenery Tweedy's Meadow Stable, making Secretariat a stablemate of that year's Kentucky Derby and Belmont Stakes winner, Riva Ridge.

I had seen Secretariat just a week before. I had been at the Meadow Stable barn one morning, checking on Riva Ridge, when exercise rider Jimmy Gaffney took me aside and said, "You wanna see the best-lookin' 2-year-old you've ever seen?"

We padded up the shed to the colt's stall. Gaffney stepped inside. "What do you think?" he asked. The horse looked magnificent, to be sure, a bright red chestnut with three white feet and a tapered white marking down his face. "He's gettin' ready," Gaffney said. "Don't forget the name: Secretariat. He can run." And then, conspiratorially, Gaffney whispered, "Don't quote me, but this horse will make them all forget Riva Ridge."

So that is where I had first seen him, and here he was in the second at Aqueduct. I rarely bet in those days, but Secretariat was 3–1, so I put $10 on his nose. Florio and I fixed our binoculars on him and watched it all. Watched him as he was shoved sideways at the break, dropping almost to his knees, when a colt named Quebec turned left out of the gate and crashed into him. Saw him blocked in traffic down the back side and shut off again on the turn for home. Saw him cut off a second time deep in the stretch as he was making a final run. Saw him finish fourth, obviously much the best horse, beaten by only 1¼ lengths after really running but an eighth of a mile.

You should have seen Clem. Smashing his binoculars down on his desk, he leaped to his feet, banged his chair against the wall behind him, threw a few punches in the air and bellowed, "Secretariat! That's my Derby horse for next year!"

Two weeks later, when the colt raced to his first victory by six, Florio announced to all the world, "Secretariat will win the Triple Crown next year." He nearly got into a fistfight in the Aqueduct press box that day when Mannie Kalish, a New York handicapper, chided him for making such an outrageously bold assertion: "Ah, you Maryland guys, you come to New York and see a horse break his maiden and think he's another Citation. We see horses like Secretariat all the time. I bet he don't even *run* in the Derby." Stung by the put-down "you Maryland guys," Florio came forward and stuck his finger into Kalish's chest, but two writers jumped between them, and they never came to blows.

The Secretariat phenomenon, with all the theater and passion that would attend it, had begun. Florio was right, of course, and by the end of Secretariat's 2-year-old season, everyone else who had seen him perform knew it. All you had to do was watch the Hopeful Stakes at Saratoga. I was at the races that August afternoon with Arthur Kennedy, an old-time racetracker and handicapper who had been around the horses since the 1920s, and even he had never seen anything quite like it. Dropping back to dead last out of the gate, Secretariat trailed eight horses into the far turn, where jockey Ron Turcotte swung him to the outside. Three jumps past the half-mile pole the colt exploded. "Now he's runnin'!" Kennedy said.

You could see the blue-and-white silks as they disappeared behind one horse, reappeared in a gap between horses, dropped out of sight again and finally reemerged as Secretariat powered to the lead off the turn. He dashed from last to first in 290 yards, blazing through a quarter in :22, and galloped home in a laugher to win by six. It was a performance with style, touched by art. "I've never seen a 2-year-old do that," Kennedy said quietly. "He looked like a 4-year-old out there."

So that was when I knew. The rest of Secretariat's 2-year-old campaign—in which he lost only once, in the Champagne Stakes, when he was disqualified from first to second after bumping Stop the Music at the top of the stretch—was simply a mopping-up operation. At year's end, so dominant had he been that he became the first 2-year-old to be unanimously voted Horse of the Year.

Secretariat wintered at Hialeah, preparing for the Triple Crown, while I shoveled snow in Huntington, N.Y., waiting for him to race again. In February, 23-year-old Seth Hancock, the new president of Claiborne Farm, announced that he had syndicated the colt as a future breeding stallion for $6.08 million, then a world record, in 32 shares at $190,000 a share, making the 1,154-pound horse worth more than three times his weight in gold. (Bullion was selling at the time for $90 an ounce.) Like everyone else, I thought Secretariat would surely begin his campaign in Florida, and I did not expect to see him again until the week before the Kentucky Derby. I was browsing through a newspaper over breakfast one day when I saw a news dispatch whose message went through me like a current. Secretariat would be arriving soon to begin his Triple Crown campaign by the way of the three New York prep races: the Bay Shore, the Gotham and the Wood Memorial Stakes.

"Hot damn!" I blurted to my family. "Secretariat is coming to New York!"

At the time I had in mind doing a diary about the horse, a chronicle of the adventures of a Triple Crown contender, which I thought might one day make a magazine piece. The colt arrived at Belmont Park on March 10, and the next day I was there at 7 A.M., scribbling notes in a pad. For the next 40 days, in what became a routine, I would fall out of bed at 6 A.M., make a cup of instant coffee, climb into my rattling green Toyota and drive the 20 miles to Belmont Park. I had gotten to know the Meadow Stable family—Tweedy, Laurin, Gaffney, groom Eddie Sweat, assistant trainer Henny Hoeffner—in my tracking of Riva Ridge the year before, and I had come to feel at home around Belmont's Barn 5, particularly around stall 7, Secretariat's place. I took no days off, except one morning to hide Easter eggs, and I spent hours sitting on the dusty floor outside Secretariat's stall, talking to Sweat as he turned a rub rag on the colt, filled his water bucket, bedded his stall with straw, kept him in hay and oats. I took notes compulsively, endlessly, feeling for the texture of the life around the horse.

A typical page of scribblings went like this: "Sweat talks to colt . . . easy, Red, I'm comin' in here now . . . stop it, Red! You behave now. . . . Sweat moves around colt. Brush in hand. Flicks off dust. Secretariat sidesteps and pushes Sweat. Blue Sky. Henny comes up, 'How's he doin', Eddie?' 'He's gettin' edgy.' . . . Easy Sunday morning."

Secretariat was an amiable, gentlemanly colt, with a poised and playful nature that at times made him seem as much a pet as the stable dog was. I was standing in front of his stall one morning, writing, when he reached out, grabbed my notebook in his teeth and sank back inside, looking to see what I would do. "Give the man his notebook back!" yelled Sweat. As the groom dipped under the webbing, Secretariat dropped the notebook on the bed of straw.

Another time, after raking the shed, Sweat leaned the handle of the rake against the stall webbing and turned to walk away. Secretariat seized the handle in his mouth and began pushing and pulling it across the floor. "Look at him rakin' the shed!" cried Sweat. All up and down the barn, laughter fluttered like the pigeons in the stable eaves as the colt did a passable imitation of his own groom.

By his personality and temperament, Secretariat became the most engaging character in the barn. His own stable pony, a roan named Billy Silver, began an unrequited love affair with him. "He loves Secretariat, but Secretariat don't pay any attention to him," Sweat said one day. "If Billy sees you grazin' Secretariat, he'll go to hollerin' until you bring him out. Secretariat just ignores him. Kind of sad, really." One morning, I was walking beside Hoeffner through the shed, with Gaffney and Secretariat ahead of us, when Billy stuck his head out of his jerry-built stall and nuzzled the colt as he went by.

Hoeffner did a double take. "Jimmy!" he yelled. "Is that pony botherin' the big horse?"

"Nah," said Jimmy. "He's just smellin' him a little."

Hoeffner's eyes widened. Spinning around on his heels, jabbing a finger in the air, he bellowed, "Get the pony out of here! I don't want him smellin' the big horse."

Leaning on his rake, Sweat laughed softly and said, "Poor Billy Silver. He smelled the wrong horse!"

I remember wishing that those days could breeze on forever—the mornings over coffee and doughnuts at the truck outside the barn, the hours spent watching the red colt walk to the track and gallop once around, the days absorbing the rhythms of the life around the horse. I had been following racehorses since I was 12, back in the days of Native Dancer, and now I was an observer on an odyssey, a quest for the Triple Crown. It had been 25 years since Citation had won racing's Holy Grail. But for me the adventure really began in the early morning of March 14, when Laurin lifted Turcotte aboard Secretariat and said, "Let him roll, Ronnie."

The colt had filled out substantially since I had last seen him under tack, in the fall, and he looked like some medieval charger—his thick neck bowed and his chin drawn up beneath its mass, his huge shoulders shifting as he strode, his coat radiant and his eyes darting left and right. He was walking to the track for his final workout, a three-eighths-of-a-mile drill designed to light the fire in him for the seven-furlong Bay Shore Stakes three days later. Laurin, Tweedy and I went to the clubhouse fence near the finish line, where we watched and waited as Turcotte headed toward the pole and let Secretariat rip. Laurin clicked his stopwatch.

The colt was all by himself through the lane, and the sight and sound of him racing toward us is etched forever in memory: Turcotte was bent over him, his jacket blown up like a parachute, and the horse was reaching out with his forelegs in that distinctive way he had, raising them high and then, at the top of the lift, snapping them out straight and with tremendous force, the snapping hard as bone, the hooves striking the ground and folding it beneath him. Laurin clicked his watch as Secretariat raced under the wire. "Oh, my god!" he cried. "Thirty-three and three-fifths!" Horses rarely break 34 seconds in three-furlong moves.

Looking ashen, fearing the colt might have gone too fast, Laurin headed for the telephone under the clubhouse to call the upstairs clocker, Jules Watson: "Hello there, Jules. How fast did you get him?"

I watched Laurin's face grow longer as he listened, until he looked thunderstruck: *"Thirty-two and three fifths?"* A full second faster than Laurin's own clocking, it was the fastest three-furlong workout I had ever heard of. Tweedy smiled cheerily and said, "Well, that ought to open his pipes!"

Oh, it did that. Three days later, blocked by a wall of horses in the Bay Shore, Secretariat plunged through like a fullback, 220 yards from the wire, and bounded off to win the race by 4½ lengths. I could hear a man screaming behind me. I turned and saw Roger Laurin, Lucien's son, raising his arms in the air and shouting, "He's too much horse! They can't stop him. They can't even stop him with a wall of horses!"

I had ridden horses during my youth in Morton Grove, Ill., and I remember one summer I took a little black bullet of a thoroughbred filly out of the barn and walked her to the track that rimmed the polo field across Golf Road. I had been to the races a few times, had seen the jockeys ride, and I wanted to feel what it was like. So I hitched up my stirrups and galloped her around the east turn, standing straight up. Coming off the turn, I dropped into a crouch and clucked to her. She took off like a sprinter leaving the blocks—

swoooosh!—and the wind started whipping in my eyes. I could feel the tears streaming down my face, and then I looked down and saw her knees pumping like pistons. I didn't think she would make the second turn, the woods were looming ahead, big trees coming up, and so I leaned a little to the left, and she made the turn before she started pulling up. No car ever took me on a ride like that. And no roller coaster, either. Running loose, without rails, she gave me the wildest, most thrilling ride I had ever had.

But that was nothing like the ride Secretariat gave me in the 12 weeks from the Bay Shore through the Belmont Stakes. Three weeks after the Bay Shore, Turcotte sent the colt to the lead down the backstretch in the one-mile Gotham. It looked like they were going to get beat when Champagne Charlie drove to within a half length at the top of the stretch—I held my breath—but Turcotte sent Secretariat on, and the colt pulled away to win by three, tying the track record of 1:33⅗.

By then I had begun visiting Charles Hatton, a columnist for the *Daily Racing Form* who the previous summer had proclaimed Secretariat the finest physical specimen he had ever seen. At 67, Hatton had seen them all. After my morning work was over, I would trudge up to Hatton's private aerie at Belmont Park and tell him what I had learned. I was his backstretch eyes, he my personal guru. One morning Hatton told me that Secretariat had galloped a quarter mile past the finish line at the Gotham, and the clockers had timed him pulling up at 1:59⅖, three fifths of a second faster than Northern Dancer's Kentucky Derby record for 1¼ miles.

"This sucker breaks records pulling up," Hatton said. "He might be the best racehorse I ever saw. Better than Man o' War."

Those were giddy, heady days coming to the nine-furlong Wood Memorial, the colt's last major prep before the Kentucky Derby. On the day of the Wood, I drove directly to Aqueduct and spent the hour before the race in the receiving barn with Sweat, exercise rider Charlie Davis and Secretariat. When the voice over the loudspeaker asked the grooms to ready their horses, Sweat approached the colt with the bridle. Secretariat always took the bit easily, opening his mouth when Sweat moved to fit it in, but that afternoon it took Sweat a full five minutes to bridle him. Secretariat threw his nose in the air, backed up, shook his head. After a few minutes passed, I asked, "What's wrong with him, Eddie?"

Sweat brushed it off: "He's just edgy."

In fact, just that morning, Dr. Manuel Gilman, the track veterinarian, had lifted the colt's upper lip to check his identity tattoo and had discovered a painful abscess about the size of a quarter. Laurin decided to run Secretariat anyway—the colt needed the race—but he never told anyone else about the boil. Worse than the abscess, though, was the fact that Secretariat had had the feeblest workout of his career four days earlier when Turcotte, seeing a riderless horse on the track, had slowed the colt to protect him from a collision. Secretariat finished the mile that day in 1:42⅗, five seconds slower than Laurin wanted him to go. Thus he came to the Wood doubly compromised.

The race was a disaster. Turcotte held the colt back early, but when he tried to get Secretariat to pick up the bit and run, he got no response. I could see at the far turn that the horse was dead. He never made a race of it, struggling to finish third, beaten by four lengths by his own stablemate, Angle Light, and by Sham. Standing near the owner's box, I saw Laurin turn to Tweedy and yell, "Who won it?"

"You won it!" Tweedy told him.

"Angle Light won it," I said to him.

"Angle Light?" he howled back.

But of course! Laurin trained him, too, and so Laurin had just won the Wood, but with the wrong horse.

I was sick. All those hours at the barn, all those early mornings at the shed, all that time and energy for naught. And in the most important race of his career, Secretariat had come up as hollow as a gourd. The next two weeks were among the most agonizing of my life. As great a stallion as he was, Bold Ruler had been essentially a speed sire and had never produced a single winner of a Triple Crown race. I couldn't help but suspect that Secretariat was another Bold Ruler, who ran into walls beyond a mile. In the next two weeks Churchill Downs became a nest of rumors that Secretariat was unsound. Jimmy (the Greek) Snyder caused an uproar when he said the colt had a bum knee that was being treated with ice packs. I *knew* that wasn't true. I had been around Secretariat all spring, and the most ice I had seen near him was in a glass of tea.

All I could hope for, in those final days before the Derby, was that the colt had been suffering from a bellyache on the day of the Wood and had not been up to it. I remained ignorant of the abscess for weeks, and I had not yet divined the truth about Secretariat's training: He needed hard, blistering workouts before he ran, and that slow mile before the Wood had been inadequate. The night before the Derby, I made my selections for the newspaper, and the next day, two hours before post time, I climbed the stairs to the Churchill Downs jockeys' room to see Turcotte. He greeted me in an anteroom, looking surprisingly relaxed. Gilman had taken him aside a few days earlier and told him of the abscess. Turcotte saw that the boil had been treated and had disappeared. The news had made him euphoric, telling him all he needed to know about the Wood.

"You nervous?" he asked.

I shrugged. "I don't think you'll win," I said. "I picked My Gallant and Sham one-two, and you third."

"I'll tell you something," Turcotte said. "He'll beat these horses if he runs his race."

"What about the Wood?" I asked.

He shook me off. "I don't believe the Wood," he said. "I'm telling you. Something was wrong. But he's O.K. now. That's all I can tell you."

I shook his hand, wished him luck and left. Despite what Turcotte had said, I was resigned to the worst, and Secretariat looked hopelessly beaten as the field of 13 dashed past the finish line the first time. He was dead last. Transfixed, I could not take my eyes off him. In the first turn Turcotte swung him to the outside, and Secretariat began passing horses, and down the back side I watched the jockey move him boldly from eighth to seventh to sixth. Secretariat was fifth around the far turn and gaining fast on the outside. I began chanting, "Ride him, Ronnie! Ride him!" Sham was in front, turning for home, but then there was Secretariat, joining him at the top of the stretch. Laffit Pincay, on Sham, glanced over and saw Secretariat and went to the whip. Turcotte lashed Secretariat. The two raced head and head for 100 yards, until gradually Secretariat pulled away. He won by 2½ lengths. The crowd roared, and I glanced at the tote board: 1:59⅖! A new track and Derby record.

Throwing decorum to the wind, I vaulted from my seat and dashed madly through the press box, jubilantly throwing a fist in the air. Handicapper Steve Davidowitz came racing toward me from the other end. We clasped arms and spun a jig in front of the copy machine. "Unbelievable!" Davidowitz cried.

I bounded down a staircase, three steps at a time. Turcotte had dismounted and was crossing the racetrack when I reached him. "What a ride!" I yelled.

"What did I tell you, Mr. Bill?" he said.

I had just witnessed the greatest Kentucky Derby performance of all time. Secretariat's quarter-mile splits were unprecedented—:25⅕, :24, :23⅘, :23⅖ and :23. He ran each quarter faster than the preceding one. Not even the most veteran racetracker could recall a horse who had done this in a mile-and-a-quarter race. As quickly as his legions (I among them) had abandoned him following the Wood, so did they now proclaim Secretariat a superhorse.

We all followed him to Pimlico for the Preakness two weeks later, and he trained as if he couldn't get enough of it. He thrived on work and the racetrack routine. Most every afternoon, long after the crowds had dispersed, Sweat would graze the colt on a patch of grass outside the shed, then lead him back into his stall and while away the hours doing chores. One afternoon I was folded in a chair outside the colt's stall when Secretariat came to the door shaking his head and stretching his neck, curling his upper lip like a camel does. "What's botherin' you, Red?" Sweat asked. The groom stepped forward, plucked something off the colt's whiskers and blew it into the air. "Just a pigeon feather itchin' him," said Sweat. The feather floated into the palm of my hand. So it ended up in my wallet, along with the $2 pari-mutuel ticket that I had on Secretariat to win the Preakness.

In its own way Secretariat's performance in the 1³⁄₁₆-mile Preakness was even more brilliant than his race in the Derby. He dropped back to last out of the gate, but as the field dashed into the first turn, Turcotte nudged his right rein as subtly as a man adjusting his cuff, and the colt took off like a flushed deer. The turns at Pimlico are tight, and it had always been considered suicidal to take the first bend too fast, but Secretariat sprinted full-bore around it, and by the time he turned into the back side, he was racing to the lead. Here Turcotte hit the cruise control. Sham gave chase in vain, and Secretariat coasted home to win by 2½. The electric timer malfunctioned, and Pimlico eventually settled on 1:54⅖ as the official time, but two *Daily Racing Form* clockers caught Secretariat in 1:53⅖, a track record by three fifths of a second.

I can still see Clem Florio shaking his head in disbelief. He had seen thousands of Pimlico races and dozens of Preaknesses but never anything like this. "Horses don't *do* what he did here today," he kept saying. "They just don't *do* that and win."

Secretariat wasn't just winning. He was performing like an original, making it all up as he went along. And everything was moving so fast, so unexpectedly, that I was having trouble keeping a perspective on it. Not three months before, after less than a year of working as a turf writer, I had started driving to the racetrack to see this one horse. For weeks I was often the only visitor there, and on many afternoons it was just Sweat, the horse and me in the fine dust with the pregnant stable cat. And then came the Derby and the Preakness, and two weeks later the colt was on the cover of *Time, Sports Illustrated* and *Newsweek,* and he was a staple of the morning and evening news. Secretariat suddenly transcended horse racing and became a cultural phenomenon, a sort of undeclared national holiday from the tortures of Watergate and the Vietnam War.

I threw myself with a passion into that final week before the Belmont. Out to the barn every morning, home late at night, I became almost manic.

The night before the race I called Laurin at home, and we talked for a long while about the horse and the Belmont. I kept wondering, What is Secretariat going to do for an encore? Laurin said, "I think he's going to win by more than he has ever won in his life. I think he'll win by 10."

I slept at the *Newsday* offices that night, and at 2 A.M. I drove to Belmont Park to begin my vigil at the barn. I circled around to the back of the shed, lay down against a tree and fell asleep. I awoke to the crowing of a cock and watched as the stable workers showed up. At 6:07 Hoeffner strode into the shed, looked at Secretariat and called out to Sweat, "Get the big horse ready! Let's walk him about 15 minutes."

Sweat slipped into the stall, put the lead shank on Secretariat and handed it to Charlie Davis, who led the colt to the outdoor walking ring. In a small stable not 30 feet away, pony girl Robin Edelstein knocked a water bucket against the wall. Secretariat, normally a docile colt on a shank, rose up on his hind legs, pawing at the sky, and started walking in circles. Davis cowered below, as if beneath a thunderclap, snatching at the chain and begging the horse to come down. Secretariat floated back to earth. He danced around the ring as if on springs, his nostrils flared and snorting, his eyes rimmed in white.

Unaware of the scene she was causing, Edelstein rattled the bucket again, and Secretariat spun in a circle, bucked and leaped in the air, kicking and spraying cinders along the walls of the pony barn. In a panic Davis tugged at the shank, and the horse went up again, higher and higher, and Davis bent back, yelling "Come on down! Come on down!"

I stood in awe. I had never seen a horse so fit. The Derby and Preakness had wound him as tight as a watch, and he seemed about to burst out of his coat. I had no idea what to expect that day in the Belmont, with him going a mile and a half, but I sensed we would see more of him than we had ever seen before.

Secretariat ran flat into legend, started running right out of the gate and never stopped, ran poor Sham into defeat around the first turn and down the backstretch and sprinted clear, opening two lengths, four, then five. He dashed to the three-quarter pole in 1:09⅘, the fastest six-furlong clocking in Belmont history. I dropped my head and cursed Turcotte: *What is he thinking about? Has he lost his mind?* The colt raced into the far turn, opening seven lengths past the half-mile pole. The timer flashed his astonishing mile mark: 1:34⅕!

I was seeing it but not believing it. Secretariat was still sprinting. The four horses behind him disappeared. He opened 10. Then 12. Halfway around the turn he was 14 in front . . . 15 . . . 16 . . . 17. Belmont Park began to shake. The whole place was on its feet. Turning for home, Secretariat was 20 in front, having run the mile and a quarter in 1:59 flat, faster than his Derby time.

He came home alone. He opened his lead to 25 . . . 26 . . . 27 . . . 28. As rhythmic as a rocking horse, he never missed a beat. I remember seeing Turcotte look over to the timer, and I looked over, too. It was blinking 2:19, 2:20. The record was 2:26⅘. Turcotte scrubbed on the colt, opening 30 lengths, finally 31. The clock flashed crazily: 2:22 . . . 2:23. The place was one long, deafening roar. The colt seemed to dive for the finish, snipping it clean at 2:24.

I bolted up the press box stairs with exultant shouts and there yielded a part of myself to that horse forever.

I didn't see Lawrence Robinson that day last October. The next morning I returned to Claiborne to interview Seth Hancock. On my way through the farm's offices, I saw one of the employees crying at her desk. Treading lightly, I passed farm manager John Sosby's office. I stopped, and he called me in. He looked like a chaplain whose duty was to tell the news to the victim's family.

"Have you heard about Secretariat?" he asked quietly.

I felt the skin tighten on the back of my neck. "Heard what?" I asked. "Is he all right?"

"We might lose the horse," Sosby said. "He came down with laminitis last month. We thought we had it under control, but he took a bad turn this morning. He's a very sick horse. He may not make it.

"By the way, why are you here?"

I had thought I knew, but now I wasn't sure.

Down the hall, sitting at his desk, Hancock appeared tired, despairing and anxious, a man facing a decision he didn't want to make. What Sosby had told me was just beginning to sink in. "What's the prognosis?" I asked.

"Ten days to two weeks," Hancock said.

"Two weeks? Are you serious?" I blurted.

"You asked me the question," he said.

I sank back in my chair. "I'm not ready for this," I told him.

"How do you think I feel?" he said. "Ten thousand people come to this farm every year, and all they want to see is Secretariat. They don't give a hoot about the other studs. You want to know who Secretariat is in human terms? Just imagine the greatest athlete in the world. The greatest. Now make him six foot three, the perfect height. Make him real intelligent and kind. And on top of that, make him the best-lookin' guy ever to come down the pike. He was all those things as a horse. He isn't even a horse anymore. He's a legend. So how do you think I feel?"

Before I left I asked Hancock to call me in Lexington if he decided to put the horse down. We agreed to meet at his mother's house the next morning. "By the way, can I see him?" I asked.

"I'd rather you not," he said. I told Hancock I had been to Robinson's house the day before, and I had seen Secretariat from a distance, grazing. "That's fine," Hancock said. "Remember how you saw him, that way. He doesn't look good."

Secretariat was suffering the intense pain in the hooves that is common to laminitis. That morning Anderson had risen at dawn to check on the horse, and Secretariat had lifted his head and nickered very loudly. "It was like he was beggin' me for help," Anderson would later recall.

I left Claiborne stunned. That night I made a dozen phone calls to friends, telling them the news, and I sat up late, dreading the next day. I woke up early and went to breakfast and came back to the room. The message light was dark. It was Wednesday, Oct. 4. I drove out to Dell Hancock's place in Paris. "It doesn't look good," she said. We had talked for more than an hour when Seth, looking shaken and pale, walked through the front door. "I'm afraid to ask," I said.

"It's very bad," he said. "We're going to have to put him down today."

"When?"

He did not answer. I left the house, and an hour later I was back in my room in Lexington. I had just taken off my coat when I saw it, the red blinking light on my phone. I knew. I walked around the room. Out the door and down the hall. Back into the room. Out the door and down to the lobby. Back into the room. I called sometime after noon. "Claiborne Farm called," said the message operator.

I phoned Annette Covault, an old friend who is the mare booker at Claiborne, and she was crying when she read the message: "Secretariat was euthanized at 11:45 A.M. today to prevent further suffering from an incurable condition. . . ."

The last time I remember really crying was on St. Valentine's Day 1982, when my wife called to tell me that my father had died. At the moment she called, I was sitting in a purple room in Caesars Palace, in Las Vegas, waiting for an interview with the heavyweight champion, Larry Holmes. Now here I was, in a different hotel room in a different town, suddenly feeling like a very old and tired man of 48, leaning with my back against a wall and sobbing for a long time with my face in my hands.

Nona Garson

From the New Jersey *Star-Ledger,* May 1997

BY NANCY JAFFER

Nancy Jaffer, the award-winning reporter who specializes in equestrian sports, has covered five Olympics, seven World Championships, and 16 World Cup finals. She has written the equestrian column in The New Jersey *Star Ledger* for three decades.

Since this profile was written four years ago, Nona Garson accomplished one of her primary goals when she rode Rhythmical on the United States Equestrian Team's show jumping squad at the 2000 Olympics in Sydney, Australia.

The sport of show jumping turns a glamorous face to the world, with stops in Palm Beach County, Fla., during the winter, Europe and the Hamptons during the summer. There are champagne victory celebrations and chicly outfitted wealthy patrons, necessary to supply horses that cost six figures or more.

But when the competition is over and the TV cameras leave, the top riders can't just go home and relax. Horses take seven-day-a-week dedication and endless schooling that doesn't always pay off. Despite their size, they are fragile creatures. They also have minds of their own. The frustrations resulting from that combination are endless.

Success requires many early mornings and late nights, more of which are spent on the road than at home. Most purses in U.S. competitions run between $25,000 and $50,000, with the winner's share a small portion of that. Any real money is made from training and selling horses; subsistence comes from giving lessons. A lot of time is spent wondering how to make ends meet. For every equestrian at the top of the standings, there are scores at the bottom, hoping for the right horse and the big break that will boost them out of the local circuit into the big time.

Nona Garson of Tewksbury, N.J., once knew just the flip side of show jumping's dazzle, going from the dusty rings at one small New Jersey show to the dusty rings at another, performing only for friends, family and a few interested spectators.

Still, she was fascinated by it.

"I think jumping is the biggest thrill of all. It's the closest thing to flying," said the 38-year-old equestrian, as exuberant as if she had discovered it yesterday. "Nothing feels better than galloping down to a big jump and having the horse take flight. It's like being superhuman."

Before each event, riders go into the ring without their horses and scout the layout, which is always different. In grands prix, the highest form of competition, it's not uncommon to find the jump rails standing up to 5-feet, 3-inches, and obstacles stretching more than 6 feet wide. Course designers concentrate on the distance between the fences, requiring riders to figure out how to adjust their horses' strides so they meet each of the brightly colored obstacles perfectly.

Knocking down a pole means a 4-point penalty, and the horse with the least penalties wins, usually after a timed tie-breaker.

"Some days, you walk the course and it looks impossible," said Garson, now ranked sixth in the country. "You wonder, how could you get that high in the air, but you do it. It's just such a feeling. I've been dedicated to that feeling my whole life."

She and her late father, George Garson, who was divorced when Nona was a child, moved to Tewksbury from Westfield, N.J., more than 30 years ago. "I'm the only person I know in the sport who spent my whole life in one place," said Garson, flashing her trademark perky smile.

Her farm is called The Ridge, and it commands an impressive view of Round Valley Reservoir, green fields and plenty of trees. From her 200-year-old farmhouse, painted a Colonial shade of blue, Garson can see her stables and paddocks.

That was where she began riding when she was five, on a half-wild Shetland pony named Maple Sugar. "I proceeded to fall off that pony at least three times a day, every day that I had it. I was on the ground more than I was on the pony," said Garson. That just honed her determination, forming her rough-and-ready approach. It brought success on the Jersey circuit, even if it didn't give her a reputation for being a smooth stylist.

After lessons with instructors in the area, Garson improved and won dozens of state championships, though she didn't seem destined for anything more. "She was the local girl hero. But if anybody had ever said Nona Garson would be one of the top grand prix riders in the country, I would have been amazed," said Scott Milne, a trainer who was traveling the Jersey circuit when Garson was doing well there. "I never watched her and thought, 'This girl is such a talent,' though she did have guts. She made it to the top of the jumper ranks from out of nowhere."

"You have to be patient. You have to believe," she said. "You can't get hung up on what's gone wrong. Riding is an exercise in optimism."

Her breakthrough came in the final Pan American Games trials in 1995, over a rigorous course on which many experienced riders had failed and fallen. There couldn't have been a more difficult, or controversial, victory—people had a hard time believing she had won.

She showed them all by becoming a regular in the ribbons on the grand prix circuit. Last fall, Garson took a class at the National Horse Show in Madison Square Garden. That fulfilled an ambition she had held since she was a wide-eyed little girl in Mary Jane shoes and white ankle socks, traveling to Manhattan to see the venerable show for the first time.

One of her horses, the snowy-coated Derrek, whom she owns with Toni and Leon Andors, has been brought along by Garson since he was an un-schooled two-year-old. Another, Rhythmical, is a Russian-bred with enough ability to make him one of the world's best show jumpers. She has successfully solicited friends and neighbors, like Rhythmical's co-owners, the Kamine family, to buy her horses, a must for someone without an independent fortune.

These days, her business at home is run by Liz Perry, who has taken over the 30-horse operation, where Garson trains and gives lessons when she can. She never forgets her equestrian roots, however, unlike some riders who have no interest in the small shows where they developed their skills.

After her father died in 1990, Garson decided it was the moment to see how far she could go with show jumping. "It took me a long time to figure out how to do it," she said. "I always had to make a living. Some people have the luxury of not doing that. I took a big chance, because I had a good business at home. If my dad were alive, he would not have approved."

He wouldn't have been the only one.

"I've had 100 people tell me, 'You shouldn't do this. You don't have the money, you don't have the talent, you're not going to make it.' There are always doubters, but I don't worry about what other people think." She began training with George Morris, the best known of America's instructors in the sport, and co-chef d'equipe (team manager) for show jumping with the U.S. Equestrian Team.

"Nona's very talented," observed Morris, shortly after she started working with him. "She's been a local star, but she could do very well in the big time. She's got to go to the big time and learn to 'live' there."

It wasn't an easy move.

One of the worst moments on her Florida circuit grand prix debut involved getting thrown into a water jump and having to drag herself out, dripping wet, in front of spectators and the elite riders whose ranks she was trying to join. Others might have given up, but Garson had learned not to do that from her earliest moments with Maple Sugar and his successor, a feisty mare named Peppermint.

The weekend before she went to Sweden for this month's Volvo Show Jumping World Cup finals, Garson was at a small show in Moorestown (cq), N.J., coaching riders competing in children's and adult jumper classes over fences that were miniscule, compared to what she's been jumping.

"It's nice to come back and see all the people I grew up with," said Garson, "and I still enjoy teaching."

Although she was on the bronze medal team at the 1995 Pan American Games, where she finished 12th individually, the World Cup was her biggest test so far. Practically every great rider on earth was on hand to try their luck in an arena filled with fabulous flower arrangements and an electricity generated by thousands of eager screaming, stomping Swedes.

She managed to finish 25th of 42, with several better-known riders below her in the standings. Garson has no doubt she'll be back another year and do better, while continuing to pursue her goal of riding in next year's World Equestrian Games and the 2000 Olympics.

The rider has little time for anything but horses, though she does try to take a break occasionally. She took up tennis. "It's fun to do other things, but I don't forsee myself at Wimbledon," the trim, 5-foot-2 athlete said with a sly smile. Riders' personal lives inevitably suffer with the demands of their sport. Garson was wed briefly to another trainer, but that didn't work out. "At this level, show jumping is all-consuming," she explained. "It's definitely a situation where you're married to the job."

"I tell people who don't know about show business that, 'I'm like the girl swinging on the flying trapeze in the circus. We travel from town to town and everybody stays in hotels. It's a major commitment in your life.

"Some understand it and some don't. But I have a good time and I love all the people I'm with. And I believe the right man will find me."

Her enjoyment hasn't waned with the demands of her work, or with the knowledge that she has made the big time. "On the worst day, I think I have the best job in the world. To me, it's such a treat to be able to do this," she said.

That enthusiasm is catching. Two-time World Cup winner Ian Millar of Canada is among the great riders who have learned to accept and appreciate Garson. "I have a great respect for her competitive instincts, dedication and focus," he said. "She's an inspiration for people who want to realize a dream."

The star of Garson's string is the Russian-bred Rhythmical, whom she spotted in a class for young riders two years ago in Sweden. The Russians originally sold him as part of a group of horses to a Finn—for $10,000 U.S. and 150 used washing machines. Times were bad after the collapse of the USSR, and machinery was more valuable than money.

"This horse, I'm sure if he could talk, he'd have some tales," said Garson, and shook her head. Scars and tattooed identification numbers bear mute testimony to the 12-year-old's past. While Rhythmical now travels in luxury in an enclosed van, it wasn't so long ago that he was shipped on an open truck.

In Finland, he became a lowly lesson horse. "The first people who bought him couldn't train him," explained Garson. He's difficult-natured. Nobody wanted to ride him; he's too fresh."

Her affinity for such temperaments helped her get to the root of his personality, and work from there until animal and rider bonded.

"He's a lot of horse, more powerful than the average horse," she said. Even Garson didn't realize how special he was at first, however.

"I knew I had a really good competitive horse, big-hearted and really fast. I wasn't sure how much sheer scope he had. But I thought my determination and his physical ability could make up for that, and he's risen to the occasion. I've never not had enough horse. His scope is endless; just the opposite of what you see when you look at him."

Compact and trim, his chestnut coat glinting red in the sun, Rhythmical doesn't have a special aura until he gets to the bottom of a jump, where he explodes over it like a starburst. His attributes have convinced Garson she'd like to have another Russian horse, but this is probably not the moment to go looking for one. "It's a dangerous trip right now," she noted. "He comes from the south of Russia, and it's difficult to get there. You can only fly to a certain point. Then you have to take a train or a car." And after that, she pointed out, who knows what you'll encounter.

She doesn't ever want to part with Rhythmical. But another trainer has made a standing offer: He jokingly told her he'd be happy to buy the horse for 10 VCRs.

A Royal Rip-Off at Kingdom Hill

BY DICK FRANCIS

T he thirty mystery novels by the ex-steeplechase jockey Dick Francis did more to promote racing over fences than anything this side of *National Velvet*. He also wrote a handful of short fiction. This one investigates the age-old search if not for a foolproof handicapping system then the extent to which horseplayers will go to circumvent the laws of probability.

❖

Thursday afternoon Tricksy Wilcox scratched his armpit absentmindedly and decided Claypits wasn't worth backing in the 2:30. Tricksy Wilcox sprawled in his sagging armchair with a half-drunk can of beer within comforting reach and a huge color television bringing him the blow-by-blow from the opening race of the three-day meeting at Kingdom Hill. Only mugs, he reflected complacently, would be putting in a 9 to 5 stint in the sort of July heatwave that would have done justice to the Sahara. Sensible guys like himself sat around at home with the windows open and their shirts off, letting their beards grow while the sticky afternoon waned toward opening time.

In winter Tricksy was of the opinion that only mugs struggled to travel to work through snow and sleet, while sensible guys stayed warm in front of the TV, betting on the jumpers; and in spring there was rain, and in the autumn, fog. Tricksy at 34 had brought unemployment to a fine art and considered the idea of a full honest day's work to be a joke. It was Tricksy's wife who went out in all weathers to her job in the supermarket, Tricksy's wife who paid the rent of the council flat and left the exact money for the milkman. Eleven years of Tricksy had left her cheerful, unresentful and practical. She had waited without emotion through his two nine-month spells in prison and accepted that one day would find him back there. Her dad had been in and out all through her childhood. She felt at home with the minor criminal mind.

Tricksy watched Claypits win the 2:30 with insulting ease and drank down his dented self-esteem with the last of the beer. Nothing he bloody touched, he thought gloomily, was any bloody good these days. He was distinctly short of the readies and had once or twice had to cut down on necessities like drink and cigarettes. What he wanted, now, was a nice little wheeze, a nice little tickle, to con a lot of unsuspecting mugs into opening their wallets. The scarce ticket racket, now, that had done him proud for years, until the coppers nicked him with a stack of forged duplicates in his pocket at Wimbledon. And tourists these days were too flaky by half; you couldn't sell them subscriptions to nonexistent magazines, let alone London Bridge.

He could never afterwards work out exactly what gave him the Great Bandwagon Idea. One minute he was peacefully watching the 3 o'clock at Kingdom Hill, and the next he was flooded with a breathtaking, wild and unholy glee.

He laughed aloud. He slapped his thigh. He stood up and jigged about, unable to bear, sitting down, the audacity of his thoughts.

"O Moses," he said, gulping for air. "Money for old rope. Kingdom Hill, here I come."

Tricksy Wilcox was not the most intelligent of men.

Friday morning, Major Kevin Cawdor-Jones, manager of Kingdom Hill racecourse, took his briefcase to the routine meeting of the executive committee, most of whom detested each other. Owned and run by a small private company constantly engaged in boardroom wars, the racecourse suffered from the results of spiteful internecine decisions and never made the profit it could have done.

The appointment of Cawdor-Jones was typical of the mismanagement. Third on the list of possible candidates, and far less able than one or two, he had been chosen solely to sidestep the bitter deadlock between the pro-one line up and the pro-two. Kingdom Hill in consequence acquired a mediocre administrator; and the squabbling committee usually thwarted his more sensible suggestions.

As a soldier Cawdor-Jones had been impulsive, rashly courageous and easy-going, qualities which had ensured that he had not been given the essential promotion to colonel. As a man he was lazy and likable, and as a manager soft.

The Friday meeting habitually wasted little time in coming to blows.

"Massive step-up of security," repeated Bellamy positively. "Number one priority. Starting at once. Today."

Thin and sharp-featured, Bellamy glared aggressively round the table, and Roskin as usual with drawling voice opposed him.

"Security costs money, my dear Bellamy."

Roskin spoke patronizingly, knowing that nothing infuriated Bellamy more. Bellamy's face darkened with anger, and the security of the racecourse, like so much else, was left to the outcome of a personal quarrel.

Bellamy insisted, "We need bigger barriers, specialized extra locks on all internal doors, and double the number of police. Work must start at once."

"Racecrowds are not *hooligans,* my dear Bellamy."

Cawdor-Jones inwardly groaned. He found it tedious enough already, on non-race days, to make his tours of inspection, and he was inclined anyway not to stick punctiliously to those safeguards that already existed. Bigger barriers between enclosures would mean he could no longer climb over or through, but would have to walk the long way round. More locks meant more keys, more time-wasting, more nuisance. And all presumably for the sake of frustrating the very few scroungers who tried to cross from cheaper to more expensive enclosures without paying. He thought he would much prefer the status quo.

Tempers rose around him, and voices also. He waited resignedly for a gap.

"Er . . ." he said, clearing his throat.

The heated pro-Bellamy faction and the sneering pro-Roskin clique both turned toward him hopefully. Cawdor-Jones was their mutual safety valve; except, that was, when his solution was genuinely constructive. Then they both vetoed it because they wished they'd thought of it themselves.

"A lot of extra security would mean more work for our staff," he said diffidently. "We might have to take on an extra man or two to cope with it . . . and after the big initial outlay there would always be maintenance . . . and . . . er . . . well, what real harm can anyone do to a racecourse?"

This weak oil stilled the waters enough for both sides to begin their retreat with positions and opinions intact.

"You have a point about the staff," Bellamy conceded grudgingly, knowing that two extra men would cost a great deal more than locks, and the racecourse couldn't afford them. "But I still maintain that tighter security is essential and very much overdue."

Cawdor-Jones, in his easy-going way, privately disagreed. Nothing had ever happened to date. Why should anything ever happen in the future?

The discussion grumbled on for half an hour, and nothing at all was done.

Friday afternoon, having pinched a tenner from his wife's holiday fund in the best teapot, Tricksy Wilcox went to the races. His trip was a reconnoitering mission to spy out the land, and Tricksy, walking around with greedy eyes wide-open, couldn't stop himself from chuckling. It did occur to him once or twice that his light-hearted singlehanded approach was a waste: the big boys would have had it all planned to a second and would have set their sights high in their humorless way. But Tricksy was a loner who avoided gang life on the grounds that it was too much like hard work; bossed around all the time, and with no pension rights into the bargain.

He downed half-pints of beer at various bars and wagered smallish amounts on the Tote. He looked at the horses in the parade ring and identified the jockeys whose faces he knew from TV, and he attentively watched the races. At the end of the afternoon, with modest winnings keeping him solvent, he chuckled his way home.

Friday afternoon Mrs. Angelisa Ludville sold two one-pound Tote tickets to Tricksy Wilcox, and hundreds to other people whom she knew as little. Her mind was not on her job but on the worrying pile of unpaid bills on the bookshelf at home. Life had treated her unkindly since her 50th birthday, robbing her of her looks, because of worry, and her husband, because of a blonde. Deserted, divorced and childless, she could nevertheless have adapted contentedly to life alone had it not been for the drastic drop in comfort. Natural optimism and good humor were gradually draining away in the constant grinding struggle to make shortening ends meet.

Angelisa Ludville eyed longingly the money she took through her Tote window. Wads of the stuff passed through her hands each working day, and only a fraction of what the public wasted on gambling would, she felt, solve all her problems handsomely. But honesty was a lifetime habit; and besides, stealing from the Tote was impossible. The takings for each race were collected and checked immediately. Theft would be instantly revealed. Angelisa sighed and tried to resign herself to the imminent cutting off of her telephone.

Saturday morning, Tricksy Wilcox dressed himself carefully for the job in hand. His wife, had she not been stacking baked beans in the supermarket, would have advised against the fluorescent orange socks. Tricksy, seeing his image in the bedroom mirror only as far down as the knees, was confident that the dark suit, dim tie and bowler hat gave him the look of a proper race-going gent. He had even, without reluctance, cut two inches off his hair and removed a flourishing moustache. Complete with outsize binoculars case slung over his shoulder, he smirked at his transformation with approval and set out with a light step to catch the train to Kingdom Hill.

On the racecourse Major Kevin Cawdor-Jones made his race-day round of inspection with his usual lack of thoroughness. Slipshod holes in his management resulted also in the police contingent's arriving half an hour late and under strength; and not enough racecards had been ordered from the printers.

"Not to worry," said Cawdor-Jones, shrugging it off easily.

Mrs. Angelisa Ludville traveled to the course in the Tote's own coach, along with 50 colleagues. She looked out of the window at the passing suburbs and thought gloomily about the price of electricity. Saturday afternoon at 2:30 she was immersed in the routine of issuing tickets and taking money, concentrating on her work and feeling reasonably happy. She arranged before her the fresh batch of tickets, those for the 3 o'clock, the biggest race of the meeting. The extra-long queues would be forming soon outside, and speed and efficiency in serving the bettors was not only her job but, indeed, her pride.

At 2:55 Cawdor-Jones was in his office next to the weighing room trying to sort out a muddle over the day laborers' pay. At 2:57 the telephone at his elbow rang for about the 20th time in the past two hours, and he picked up the receiver with his mind still on the disputed hourly rates due to the stickers-back of kicked-up chunks of turf.

"Cawdor-Jones," he announced himself automatically.

A man with an Irish accent began speaking quietly.

"What?" said Cawdor-Jones. "Speak up, can't you. There's too much noise here. . . . I can't hear you."

The man with the Irish accent repeated his message in the same soft half-whisper.

"What?" said Cawdor-Jones. But his caller had rung off.

"Oh, my God," said Cawdor-Jones, and stretched a hand to the switch that connected him to the internal broadcasting system. He glanced urgently at the clock. Its hands clicked round to 2:59, and at that moment the 14 runners for the 3 o'clock race were being led into the starting stalls.

"Ladies and gentlemen," said Cawdor-Jones, his voice reverberating from every loud-speaker on the racecourse. "We have been warned that a bomb has been placed somewhere in the stands. Would you please all leave at once and go over to the center of the course while the police arrange a search."

The moment of general shock lasted less than a second. Then the huge race-crowd streamed like a river down from the steps, up from the tunnels, out of the doors, running, pelting, elbowing toward the safety of the open spaces on the far side of the track.

Bars emptied dramatically with half-full glasses overturned and smashed in the panic. The Tote queues melted instantaneously, and the ticket-sellers followed them helter-skelter. The stewards vacated their high box at a dignified downhill rush, and the racing press pell-melled for the exit without hanging about to alert their papers. City editors could wait half an hour. Bombs wouldn't.

The scrambling thousands deserted all the racecourse buildings within a space of two minutes. Only a very few stayed behind, and chief of those was Kevin Cawdor-Jones, who had never lacked for personal courage and now saw it as his duty as a soldier to remain at his post.

The under-strength of policemen collected bit by bit outside the weighing room, each man hiding his natural apprehension under a reassuring front. Probably another bloody hoax, they told one another. It was always a hoax. Or . . . nearly always. Their officer took charge of organizing the search and told the civilian Cawdor-Jones to remove himself to safety.

"No, no," said Cawdor-Jones. "While you look for the bomb, I'll make quite sure that everyone's out." He smiled a little anxiously and dived purposely into the weighing room.

All clear there, he thought, peering rapidly round the jockeys' washroom. All clear in the judges' box, the photofinish developing room, the kitchens, the boiler room, the Tote, the offices, the stores. He bustled from building to building, knowing all the back rooms, the nooks and crannies where some deaf member of the public might be sitting unawares.

He saw no people. He saw no bomb. He returned almost out of breath to the space outside the weighing room and awaited a report from the slower police.

Around the stands Tricksy Wilcox was putting the Great Bandwagon Idea into sloppy execution. Chuckling away internally over the memory of an Irish impersonation good enough for an entry to Actors Equity, he bustled speedily from bar to bar and in and out of doors, filling his large, empty binocular case with provender. It was amazing, he thought, giggling, how *careless* people were in a panic.

Twice he came face to face with the searching policemen.

"All clear in there, Officer," he said pompously, each time pointing back to where he had been. And each time the police gaze flickered unsuspectingly over the bowler hat, the dark suit, the dim tie. The police took him for one of the racecourse staff.

Only the orange socks stopped him getting clean away. One policeman, watching his receding back view, frowned uncertainly at the brilliant segments between trouser leg and shoe, and started slowly after him.

"Hey. . . ." he said.

Tricksy turned his head, saw the Law advancing, lost his nerve and then bolted. Tricksy was not the most intelligent of men.

Saturday afternoon precisely at 4 o'clock, Cawdor-Jones made another announcement.

"It appears the bomb warning was just another hoax. It is now safe for everyone to return to the stands."

The crowd streamed back in reverse and made for the bars. The barmaids returned to their posts and immediately raised hands and voices in a screeching chorus of affronted horror.

"Someone's pinched all the takings!"

"The cheek of it. He's taken our tips and all!"

In the various Tote buildings, the ticket sellers stood appalled. Most of the huge intake for the biggest race of the meeting had simply vanished.

Angelisa Ludville looked with utter disbelief at her own plundered cash box. White, shaking, she joined the clamor of voices. "The money's gone. . . ."

Cawdor-Jones received report after report with a face of anxious despair. He knew no doors had been locked after the stampede to the exits. He knew no security measures whatever had been taken. The racecourse wasn't equipped to deal with such a situation. The committee would undoubtedly blame him. Might even give him the sack.

At 4:30 he listened with astounded gratitude to news from the police that a man had been apprehended and was now helping to explain how his binoculars case came to be crammed to overflowing with used treasury notes, many of them bearing a fresh circular watermark resulting from the use of a wet beer glass as a paperweight.

Monday morning Tricksy Wilcox appeared gloomily before a magistrate and was remanded in custody for seven days. The Great Bandwagon Idea hadn't been so hot after all, and undoubtedly they would send him down for more than nine months this time.

Only one thought brightened his future. The police had tried all weekend to get information out of him, and he had kept his mouth tight shut. Where, they wanted to know, had he hidden the biggest part of the loot?

Tricksy said nothing.

There had only been room in the binoculars case for one tenth of the stolen money. Where had he put the bulk?

Tricksy wasn't telling.

He would get off more lightly, they said, if he surrendered the rest.

liant background, Grandpa licked Kelso, Damascus. He was put into a stall. We left.

Months went by. We didn't want to bug Virginia Martin and called only occasionally. When we got her, she said he was coming along. She was having various capable riders work him every day. The most frequent of these riders, we learned, was one Aleen Thomas. She was a New York City woman who worked for a film company and stabled her horse, Drummer, at Borderland Farm. Drummer's stall was next to that of Owen Smith, and Miss Thomas struck up an acquaintance with him when she saw his head hanging out over the half-door. Pretty soon she was up on him trying to make his gaits even steadier than they were.

"He was very green," she told me later. "But he was spook-proof. He was extremely handle-able, you could do anything with him, you could play under his legs and he'd stand. I wanted to get his front and haunches built up by stretching and shifting him. I saw he could be quite something at dressage and so I concentrated on that—it would round him out." That translated into making him get his legs under him and getting him muscled up and firmed up so that the sway-back would round out somewhat and make his way of going more smooth.

"He's a very giving horse," she told me, "very adaptive and affectionate. He likes people. He likes having the bottom of his face stroked. This is the first Thoroughbred I ever rode with consistency. It was fascinating to see him develop." Pretty soon she took him into a New Jersey dressage show. They came in third out of twenty in the class.

"Not bad!" I said.

"I wish my own horse were half as good," she said. By then she had asked Virginia Martin if the owner would pop for a new saddle and a special foam pad that would help compensate for the sway-back. Virginia called me, and I said I'd pop for anything. With his new equipment Owen Smith went on with Aleen Thomas. "I have never really galloped him," she told me, "because I don't want him really running loose. In company out on the trail, he canters in place when he's behind. He can't be doing that and then really opening up with handicapped kids on board."

"No, of course not," I said. No. He mustn't try to be first. We had lost that, he and I. That was for the horse he might have been.

In late May of 1985, seven months after we had delivered Owen Smith to Virginia, she called me. "I think you might like to come over on Memorial Day," she said.

I drove down. The weather was magnificent, sunny and warm. My garden was planted and I'd had peas from my vines. I arrived and Virginia introduced me to Barbara Glasow. "Our chief therapist," Virginia said.

"I've read some of your writings," I said. They had been reprinted in various Winslow bulletins Virginia had sent us. Mostly they had been incomprehensible to me—too scientific. "How you get into this horse business?" I asked, and she told me that hers was the familiar tale of the horse-crazy little girl. She was from Rochester's suburbs where there was no possibility of owning a nag, but she had a cousin in Connecticut who had one. Each summer she and her parents drove down to visit the cousin and cousin's parents, and Barbara as a child spent every possible minute on the cousin's horse. When she got older, she begged to stay longer in Connecticut than her parents' vacation plans permitted, but they consented, provided she earned enough money to pay for her own transportation back to Rochester. Every penny she could lay her hands on for months before the visit was put away to pay that transportation, for years.

Barbara as a child had been, she said, a tomboy type, but with a bad back that got worse. She found herself put under the care of a physical therapist who worked long hours, long years, with her. She decided in high school that she was going to be like her therapist. At Ithaca College in upstate New York, she majored in her chosen field but in fact spent more time at her outside job than in class. The job was taking care of some twenty horses in a riding stable. She did it along with another girl who also majored in physical therapy. They were juniors in 1973 when somehow they heard there was going to be a lecture in Toronto on horseback riding for the disabled. It was Christmas week. They got leave from their job and drove up to find a Santa Claus parade wending its way through the center of the city. They got caught up in it while they battled the marchers and the unfamiliar streets and got to the lecture only in time to hear the concluding words.

But Barbara had found her destiny. She went back to Ithaca and, through her final year at school, worked on her senior project: a study of what horses could do for the disabled. There wasn't much to go on, she found. In all of the United States there were maybe half a dozen places working on it. The people at those places were local therapists. There was no communicating with others on what they had picked up or figured out. Barbara borrowed a movie camera and as her senior project made a film analyzing a normal person's interaction with a horse at the sitting trot, how the horse's movements affected the rider, what kind of strengths the riding produced, what movement in what joints. She tied it all in to what riding might do for the disabled.

"With a cerebral palsy child," she told me, "things are likely to be all out of alignment. The back is round, the shoulders are bent, the hips don't line up right. The skeleton's not right anymore. But the walk of a horse, the right horse, that motion, forces the child, pushes the child, to move his body correctly. The hips and everything, just as if he were walking himself. The horse's movement makes him move correctly. It's not static like a chair. That horse motion teaches the child balance reaction and to lean and to have the freedom to bring the arms forward and back. That motion encourages the movement of the arms and brings out the child's balance.

"There is something else. Classically, the disabled are not in charge of anything. They are not expected to be responsible. Their parents don't make them do chores. Friends carry their books at school. But such a child has to learn he is not the center of the world; he exists in a family structure, a class structure. Riding teaches him self-esteem and control of himself and of something else—this animal. He must learn responsibility. What I teach is not recreational riding. I make a child feel what normal is, normal movement, through what the horse makes the child do and what he makes the horse do. The child ought to say, Oh, this is what normal feels like, this motion. Then the child matches it, his body matches it. He knows what normal is then.

"Now, do you see that boy there?" I looked. I saw a kid in blue jeans and sneakers. He wore a red shirt. He balanced himself with aluminum crutches holding his forearms and clutched in his fists. Barbara Glasow said to me that she had worked with him for a long time in her capacity as a contract specialist for the local school system. For she had gone on from Ithaca College to a community hospital doing physical therapy and then to public health agencies and then finally into private practice in Warwick where mostly on school contracts she worked exclusively with children. "I heard about Virginia Martin and Winslow a couple of years ago," she explained. She had found that while Virginia had no formal training in the new science of hippotherapy, she had good instincts. I gathered that Virginia's personality was right also. Sheltered workshop, sheltered homes, would never have attracted Virginia. She was the kind of person who hired as stable help those unlikely to be taken on elsewhere: boys in trouble with the law for joyriding in someone else's automobile; people with learning disabilities. "They got a problem, what's their problem?" seemed to be her way of looking at things.

"Now," Barbara was saying, "that boy is highly intelligent. He needs a challenge. He doesn't need a horse who's just going to follow other horses. He'll daydream. You daydream when someone else is responsible. So you can't just be a passenger, you have to plan ahead, ask, 'What do I do now?' And give you a horse who doesn't move real big, that horse'll tell you nothing. I need a horse with a big stride for that kid, a horse who'll make him put out, make him work. Owen Smith is the horse for Steven. That's Steven Jacobetz."

I looked at the kid. He was slowly limping away on his crutches, his legs dragging along the ground. His head hung to one side. He turned to look at something, and I saw that his mouth was partly open. It looked like he was half-laughing, but I couldn't be sure. He went down a stable aisle with his dragging walk and vanished. "He'll be riding in a few minutes," Barbara said. Here was a rider for Owen Smith in place of Cordero, Jorge Velasquez, Maple, Eddie Delahoussaye, Jacinto Vasquez.

I went to my horse. He was tacked up and groomed. A volunteer had just left him. I looked into his eyes. The memory of his birth and that kick came into my mind. "Been a long time," I said. Six years. I thought back to that day Gail Jones found him trapped and permanently crippled, my dear horse I loved and would always love above all others. There was a scraping sound to my right. Steven Jacobetz was coming back. "Owen Smith," I whispered. "For God's sake, be careful."

A young woman came up and stood next to me. "Talking to Owen, are you?"

"Yes."

"He's a Thoroughbred, you know," she said.

She was telling me.

"This is some horse," she said.

"He is? Why?"

"Well, this horse, he's eager, he's willing. He's straightforward and honest, you know. You ask him something and he understands. He's willing to work with you."

I told her who I was, or rather, what I was: his owner. She introduced herself as Ellie Celeste, an area woman who stabled her horse at Borderland Farm and was a Winslow volunteer. As we talked another volunteer came and opened the stall gate and led Owen Smith out. As he went by I held out my hand and it passed over the length of him from the neck to the withers and the side and to the haunches over the legs leading down to those terrible wounds made so long ago and never to vanish in this life.

He went with the volunteer into Virginia Martin's riding arena. There was a large round wooden platform in the center, perhaps fifteen feet in diameter, with a ramp for people in wheelchairs. Coming up, leaning on his mother's arm, his crutches left below, was Steven Jacobetz. There was a kid's hockey helmet on his head, strapped under his chin.

Below, on the tanbark, Barbara Glasow stood with three Winslow volunteers. Virginia Martin was on the platform with Linda Jacobetz. Owen Smith was led up to the platform. In front of it and perhaps two feet away was a shoulder-high wooden wall; it formed a kind of open-ended alleyway that would make it impossible for a horse to move sideways when a rider was getting on board. Owen Smith walked forward and into it and stood still.

Linda Jacobetz took her son's arm and moved him forward. A volunteer joined her and slowly they got Steven on board. *Riders up,* I thought to myself. They let him move his right leg over the saddle by himself. He took up the reins. He held them level with his nose. His slight body sagged to the left. His head lolled in that direction. His mouth was open and the helmet unevenly slanted sideways.

A volunteer held Owen Smith by a lead rein, not a nose chain but just a lead hooked to the bridle. The books say never lead a Thoroughbred without that chain over his nose so you can pull him down sharply and really rap him, and I have heard Louise Meryman, the chief instructor at the burnt Millbrook Combined Training Center and later at the Millbrook Equestrian Center, tell her students they should never even lead a Thoroughbred across a courtyard without a metal chain on his nose. Once an employee of ours left a nose chain off Beau Blaze, Owen Smith's brother, and he went up in the air and put her in the emergency room. The volunteer moved Owen Smith a couple of steps forward out of the alleyway formed by the wall and the side of the raised platform. Two more volunteers came forward, one on each side, to take hold of each of Steven's heels with one hand.

"Move out, Steven," Barbara Glasow ordered. The boy pushed at the horse with the heels held in the volunteers' hands, and they, the rider and the horse and the sidewalkers, got into motion. They began slowly to circle the arena, the volunteer in front holding Owen Smith by the lead rein, the other two holding Steven's heels. Mrs. Jacobetz and Virginia stood together on the wooden platform.

They went past a large mirror, the type every riding arena has, and then along the wall. "Get him closer to the wall," Barbara called, walking along behind. Steven tugged on the right rein and Owen Smith altered course. The horse's motion, and suddenly he appeared enormous to me, gigantic, was jolting the boy forward and then back; and before my eyes, in a matter of perhaps thirty or forty seconds, a minute at the most, Steven's bent body was being pushed up straight. He stopped sagging to the left and sat upright. Within two minutes his head had ceased lolling and was sitting straight on his neck.

They came past the wooden platform in that flow stately manner, the horse, the boy, the sidewalker-volunteers. "He certainly doesn't look scared," I remarked.

"We never use that word,"Virginia said in a reprimanding tone.

They circled the arena twice. "Unhook him," Barbara called, and the lead volunteer did so and stepped away. Steven Jacobetz, unafraid, was in full command. "You can let go," Barbara said to one of the heel-holding volunteers, and the boy was alone with only one sidewalker holding his left heel.

"Steven," Barbara called sharply, "ask him to go on. Wake up! Now turn him left. Left! Let him know what you want. Never let the signal wander with your hands. Don't be sloppy!"

She stepped forward into the center of the arena, directly before the boy and the horse. "Now I want you to make a circle around me," she said. "To your right. Go ahead. Do it." He pulled on the rein and slowly he circled her. "Now circle to your left and come back and make a left circle around me," she called. He came at her. "Don't run me over," she added. Everyone laughed, Linda,Virginia, the watching volunteers. He did as she had ordered.

And God took a handful of southerly wind, blew His breath over it and created the horse, the Bedouin saying goes; and among horses the Thoroughbred is second to none. Slowly this Thoroughbred, beautiful in my eyes, went on with his brave and willing rider. *And they shall be mine, saith the Lord of hosts, in that day when I make up my jewels.*

Ellie Celeste stood beside me. "This must be a very beautiful moment for you," she said gently.

I forced a smile. "My wife didn't come because she knew she'd cry," I said.

"Steven," Barbara was calling. "Go to A, turn around to the right and cross to R and turn left." He headed to the letter tacked on the wall and did as she had ordered. The volunteer walking alongside lightly holding his heel said something—a tall, young, local fellow who liked to come over and be with the horses and kids, I'd been told—and Steven ripped out a peal of laughter. He looked over to his mother standing with Virginia up on the wooden platform. His hands were no longer up at his nose's level but down in front of him where they should have been, where a horseman's hands are supposed to be.

"You see how he's rotating through the trunk?" Barbara asked me. "You see how the horse unites everything from the hip to the shoulder? He's stretching Steven, he's putting him together."

"Yes, I see," I got out. God knows this wasn't what I had dreamed for Owen Smith long ago. I had created him, to be brutally frank, to be egotistic, to reveal myself as someone who had dreamed only of my glory and my gold, as surely as the farmer creates corn by sowing the seed. My money had made him, my money bought his mother and his sire's semen; and I had nurtured her and him for eleven months of pregnancy. And I had kept him alive with Jayne and Gail and everyone else—and again I freely admit they know horses a hundred times better than I do—thought he should be put down. For this? For a crippled boy on a crippled horse?

No, never! I said to myself, watching him circle the arena with Steven directing him where to go and when to do it. I created him to go around different ovals: that great reaching one which is Belmont Park, that one which is reached by passing under Saratoga's noble trees, Aqueduct, Churchill Downs on the first Saturday of May these hundred and more years past, Santa Anita.

"Halt him, Steven," Barbara called. Steven tugged back, raising his hands much too high and losing all leverage. Owen Smith kept going. Barbara stepped forward and stopped him. It had been too much for the boy—this time.

"I can make him go forward but I can't stop him," Steven said. The words were indistinct, but understandable.

"You've got work to do, Steven," Barbara said. She looked up at him as he sat, quite straight. Like a horseman. "You have to work with this horse. This is your horse, Steven. You're going to work with him this summer and you're going to go in shows, you understand, you're going to go in shows through obstacle courses and you're going to trot him over cavalletti poles. Do you understand me?"

"Yes."

I turned away. I had dreamed great dreams. They were gone. There would never be another racehorse born in our barn. My picture with Jayne would never be in the corridor outside Belmont's Trustees' Room with that of old Mr. Woodward with Gallant Fox and young Mr. Woodward with Nashua, with Martha Gerry with Forego and Penny Chenery with Secretariat, with Vanderbilt with Native Dancer and Whitney with Tom Fool, with the owners of Seattle Slew and Spectacular Bid.

But what they had, *he* had. That desire to win, to do, to go on, to achieve, that drive and that something unknown, he had translated it into this, that beyond pain and above injury, he would do for this boy and for the others, the Down's syndrome kids, the blind, the riders with no arms or one leg—he would do what he could. Virginia had said to me once that it was her experience that horses who worked long years for her stayed healthy. When she retired them, she said, they sickened and died. They wanted, the good ones, to do things. "What's long years?" I had asked. "I've had horses working with kids who've been doing it twenty years," she said.

Twenty years? In twenty years I will be dead or very old. Jessica will be in her mid-thirties then, a mature woman. Perhaps now and then she will stop by Warwick, New York, to see the last of our horses, who never won a race, who never even ran. Who then, twenty years into the future, will remember that Cold Spring once paid forty dollars to win, or that Brave Gleam made up nearly thirty lengths from last to be up in a photo? But Owen Smith would be on helping those who needed him. And when he died, if I were still alive, or Jayne were still alive, or if Jessica still owned our place, he would come home to lie by little Birthday Girl, the playmate of his youth. We had made that clear to Virginia, and she had said she entirely understood.

"Go to C and turn to the left and go to M," Barbara was saying. Steven pushed with his heels, sitting straight, the hands right. Owen Smith went forward. I turned away and walked from the arena and down the stall aisle and outside to where my car was. Behind me the handicapped kid on the handicapped horse went on. I got to the car and started it and drove away. Behind me they went on with their work.

I had seen a hero riding a hero.

My horse was a winner, the victor, a great horse—the champion.

School Horses, the Most Important Assistants of the Instructor

BY COLONEL ALOIS PODHAJSKY

Colonel Alois Podhajsky served as director of Vienna's Spanish Riding School from 1936 to 1965. Responsible for saving the School's celebrated Lipizzaners during World War Two, he thus helped preserve the classical dressage tradition that has been nurtured and exhibited at the School since 1572. This selection from Podhajsky's *My Horses, My Teachers* offers advice that applies equally well to any breed or discipline.

During my period at the Cavalry School I had to ride the horses I have mentioned and also remounts, that is, young horses that had to be broken in. Besides, there were the school horses on which I was given one or two lessons daily and which helped me to understand even better how important the training of dressage is for every type of riding horse. In general a horse may be called a school horse if his training in dressage has reached such a degree that he is able to convey to the pupil the correct feeling for movement and balance and the subtlety of the aids. No instructor is capable of teaching this delicate language between rider and horse without the willing assistance of the horse. The young rider, eager to learn, may rely on his four-legged teacher whose importance sometimes even rises above that of the two-legged one. The privilege of learning on a school horse is an invaluable help for the rest of the rider's life. I will be forever grateful to my school horses, for I continued to learn from them when I was given no more lessons and was working on my own and also when I was instructing other riders.

A teacher will be successful with his teaching when he is understood and respected by his pupils. In much the same way a horseman will be able to learn from his horse only when he respects him as a creature and has affection for him. Since the horse cannot speak the rider must endeavor to guess his thoughts and to interpret his reactions and draw conclusions from his behaviour. Mutual understanding will also depend on how two creatures take to each other, which may be even more important between horse and rider than between human beings. Therefore the selection of a horse is a vital point in the future relationship. This knowledge, which I gained at the Cavalry School, was further extended at the Spanish Riding School.

There are horses who appeal to the rider immediately, whom he understands easily and likes in a short time. In such a case it is easy to adjust to each other; work becomes a pleasure; and success is certain to follow. But now and then a rider comes across a horse who is alien to him and whose reactions he cannot understand. He is quickly annoyed by repeated faults and naughtiness and often an aversion develops which compromises progress and success. Such an inexplicable aversion does not appear only in the rider but certainly also in the horse. This is why some horses who give nothing but trouble to one rider change completely with a new master and work with him in full harmony. The reason does not lie in the better abilities of the new rider and, therefore, must not be taken as a gauge of standards. It is the magnetism between two creatures, which cannot be explained by the intellect.

Matching horse and rider is an art founded on a profound knowledge first of all of the physical conformation, of the habits, and last but not least, of the characters of both partners. The stable masters at the royal courts of bygone days had to possess this knowledge to a high degree, for they had to choose and prepare the horses for their "highnesses." A prince had to be superior also in mastering his horse and it was unthinkable that he fight with him or lose his dignity and reputation by falling off in public. Therefore the books that the reputable riding and stable masters of old have left to us—there are only very few because not every good rider is a good writer and vice versa—are still of great value for us today. The horse still moves in the same way as always; he thinks and feels in the same fashion; and the conformation of his body is unaltered. He is the wonderful creature of nature as extolled in the Koran. The riding masters who attained such high and responsible positions had the duty and the leisure to study this product of nature profoundly. In every book on riding of those days there are detailed instructions about the horse's body and its functions, about stable management and saddles and bridles.

Today, however, few riders know their horses and the causes of their behaviour. Everything has become superficial nowadays, except technology. With machines the physical laws may not be disregarded as we often disregard the laws of nature with our animals. The well-founded doctrines of the old riding masters are frequently rejected today with the remark that these methods are old-fashioned and not applicable in our present times, which demand quick success. And what is the result of this fast training? The standard has declined until the once so beautiful movements have become caricatures of what they were. And yet a performance of the highest standard must be built up step by step and on a well-founded basis. I have learned by experience that today's riders may indeed rely upon the teachings of our predecessors, for they are of invaluable help in the reasonable development of this sport. If a rider thinks that he has found a new method he may be sure that if it is any good he has come upon it by instinct or by chance and that it was practiced long ago by the old masters.

Speed at the cost of quality is always wrong, not only in riding. When the famous New York City Ballet performed in Vienna I asked the ballet master George Balanchine whether he would take the so-called modern conception into consideration when training his dancers and shorten the time of their education. Excitedly Balanchine jumped off his seat and exclaimed: "How could I? The human body is still the same as always. The old schools of ballet demanded a certain amount of time and they were right. Did they not achieve perfection and have they not been our ideals for hundreds of years? Why should we change?" It is exactly the same with equitation if it pretends to be an art.

But let us go back to a small part of this art, to the choice of the right horse for the right rider, which is a sort of matchmaking between the two creatures, and should be one of the most important concerns of any good riding instructor. Unfortunately only a few of my instructors possessed this tact. In most cases the horses were allotted in a rather superficial way. Very frequently the horses were exchanged in accordance with the obvious principle of giving the difficult horse to the more accomplished rider, which would have been the correct method had it not been for the fact that as soon as the difficult horse had been somewhat retrained by the good rider, he was returned to a weaker one. In a short time there were new difficulties and the vicious circle began again. This method made the riders lose interest and pleasure in their work and did not allow a friendship to grow between horse and rider. The horse as a teacher did not come into action.

Because of these frequent changes I remember only a few school horses from my time at the Cavalry School. My first experience was a negative one and rather discouraging. From the chestnut mare Fanny I learned how vital it is for successful cooperation that the two partners be sympathetic to each other and how dismal may be the daily lesson if horse and rider do not meet in friendship. As with every school horse, I had to ride her without stir-rups for several months. I did not succeed, however, in finding contact with her and my vexation grew when, every day, she gave me trouble, unseating me by sudden leaps and starts at the most unexpected moment and at the slightest provocation. I could not discover the reason for her behaviour or bring about a change by calming her or administering punishment. With every new day it became harder to remain patient. Eventually I took such a dislike to her that I began to be annoyed the very moment she was brought into the arena. Very probably she disliked me as much as I did her; there was just no getting along with each other. And Fanny of all horses I had to keep for such a long time! But even those nerve-wracking fights had a positive result. I learned that the willing cooperation of our horses is not to be taken for granted and began to pay greater attention to the psychological relationship between horse and rider. This approach has been of great help to me in my later career as a rider as well as an instructor.

Even though I was not able to get along with Fanny I grew conscious of the fact that horses cannot all be trained after the same set pattern. The phlegmatic horse should be taken with a firmer hand and the willing horse, in-clined to nervousness, should be treated more leniently. Between the two there are a number of nuances, of course, and I realized these contrasts especially when changing from a lazy horse to a temperamental one and vice versa. Clinging to habits as every human being does, I applied the aids in the same manner and was surprised by the results. While the first horse's nervousness grew into excitement, the same degree of aids did not get the other going. As it is vital for correct and successful work to know one's partner intimately I adopted the habit, later, of eliminating difficult exercises when first riding a new horse. We are indulging our human vanity if we produce difficult airs and figures with an unknown horse. So I have also taught my pupils to take time to get to know their partners and also to give the horse time to grow accustomed to a new rider. I learned how to study the horse's movements, his suppleness and sensitiveness to the aids. I took time to understand his temperament, his character, and his capacity to learn. The horse should have the opportunity to grow accustomed to the difference in weight of a new rider, which might even be distributed in a different way, and also to the different nuances in the appli-cation of the aids so that they are understood completely. Horse and rider *must* first of all understand each other in the language of the aids before they can find understanding in the balance, rhythm, and tempo that are necessary for the harmony they should strive to achieve.

Rarely, and never in later years, did I allow the spectators to infringe upon this necessary period of getting to know each other, even if the unlookers were waiting eagerly to see how the horse—sometimes it was even their own—would go under the new rider. Nothing can prevent me now from riding an indifferent horse briskly forward in order to awaken him by changes of speed and make him take pleasure in his own movement. An excitable horse I calm by steady and almost sleepy work and coax him into finding his mental balance, which is as important to animals as it is to humans. By this careful investigation rather than with some spectacular exercises I am able to decide on the appropriate intensity of the aids, learn about the strong and weak points of the new partner, and can build up the training progressively. It enables me to reach my goal more successfully and more quickly than by rushing ahead. Having laid the foundation of confidence and friendship in this preparatory period, I have my horse "there" when I begin with the real work.

One should also consider the differing attitudes of different horses towards rewards and punishments. The tender little soul blissfully accepts the smallest caress, as was the case with Neapolitano Africa, who would have purred like a kitten had he not been a Lipizzaner stallion. The slightest rebuke, however, was a tragedy for him and he became nervous and anxious. The more materialistic horse obviously prefers sugar or other titbits to patting and stroking as if he would say: "Don't make all that fuss, go ahead and give me the sugar!" In most cases such a horse is much less impressed by a reprimand and easily digests a much stronger one. This knowledge of character is an important part in the education of a horse and a sound foundation for successful cooperation.

As I have mentioned, not every school horse is necessarily suitable for dressage competitions, but at the Cavalry School each dressage horse had to be used as a school horse outside the season of horse shows. In the second year of my appointment there I was lucky to have as my riding instructor Major Jaich, who was a successful dressage rider himself. He limited to a minimum the unpleasant changes of horses and riders and had great ability as a teacher. He was an excellent instructor who directed with tact and whose knowledge and method had sprung from practical experience. His best assistant was my school horse Greif. The two of them enriched and consolidated my equestrian knowledge to a great extent.

Greif was a big strong chestnut gelding with great intelligence and docility. Although his paces were not too brilliant, he ranked among the best school horses and was chosen to participate in the dressage competitions at the forthcoming horse shows in the spring of 1930. Thus a definite goal was given to my training and I accumulated valuable experiences in these lessons. Under the expert instruction of Major Jaich, Greif grew into an excellent teacher who took me through the dressage training up to the standard of a difficult class. On his back I learned lateral work in all paces, flying changes at every second stride, and pirouettes. The rider can learn these exercises only in this practical way and not from explanations of even the best instructor.

First of all I learned from this well-trained school horse that with riding the regularity of the movements has the same importance as the rhythm in music. To begin with I had to learn to feel this regularity and then to realize the difference whenever it changed and apply the correct means to regain this most beautiful feeling a horse can convey to his rider. Whenever his steps became irregular I could clearly feel it in the movement of his back and would then ride him briskly forward at a rising trot until he had regained his balance. When he made hasty steps I had to reduce his speed until tempo and rhythm were again regular. The most important thing was to take care not to disturb his balance with my seat. In this way I was able to maintain the same rhythm on the straight line as in lateral work. In lateral work the horse moves forward and sideways and his legs cross each other. It is a frequent fault in this movement that the horse either increases or decreases his speed. When I succeeded at last in maintaining the same rhythm whether increasing or decreasing the tempo and was able to bring about this difference by lengthening or shortening the horse's strides instead of making them faster or slower, I began to feel the full harmony of all movements. This difference of length in the horse's stride in the different speeds while the same rhythm is maintained gives brilliance to riding just as *fortissimo* and *pianissimo* give brilliance to music.

It was Greif who made me understand the flying change, that is, the flying change of lead in which the horse changes from, say, the canter right to the canter left without intermediate steps. The term right or left canter refers to the leading foreleg. For example, if the left foreleg is the one that reaches out, we speak about a canter left. Greif taught me that the rider should not attempt to indicate this change of lead to the horse by twisting his body or throwing it from one side to the other but by quietly changing the aids of leg and reins, on the condition—and this was the most important thing—that the horse moves in a lively collected canter. Thus Greif made me consider more seriously the basic gymnastic schooling of the horse, which is the foundation for more advanced training. If it is neglected, numerous difficulties will arise that will eventually hinder progress.

After a while I was able to induce Greif to execute a flying change without my aids being noticeable to the onlooker and to increase the difficulty of the exercise by repeating it after a given number of strides until Greif made a flying change after every other stride. If with all my other dressage horses later on I seemed to achieve flying changes without an apparent effort, I am indebted to Greif and the experience I gained in my work with him, which taught me never to neglect the basic schooling, i.e., the correct development of the paces.

Greif taught me also how easy it is to achieve pirouettes if the horse is in full balance. A well-balanced horse should maintain the regularity of his steps even in the smallest turns and in the pirouette should not change the rhythm of the canter but turn in regular bounds around the inside hind leg. If he loses his balance and consequently his rhythm, we have proof that the horse was not ready for this difficult exercise. The rider should concentrate again on cultivating the basic paces and ride briskly forward, executing changes of speed and small and large circles. He should practice extension and collection until the horse maintains the rhythm and the regularity of his stride even in small and smaller turns and voltes. Thanks to Greif again, there were never difficulties with my own dressage horses in the following years. After the conscientious preparation of the foundation, these difficult exercises seemed to drop into my lap like ripe fruit. And the success of my cooperation with Greif became apparent not only in my enriched experiences but also in the numerous trophies we won in various horse shows.

The second horse that I rode under the direction of Major Jaich was Jodo, a very good-looking chestnut gelding from the federal stud farm. He was the first horse that I had trained all by myself, beginning with the young remount and proceeding up to the standard of a school and dressage horse. Jodo was full of temperament and good will and he learned quickly and easily, but he had to be given enough time to understand what was required of him. Above all I had to be careful not to make him nervous. As a young rider I was full of zeal and ambition to achieve noticeable progress and so it happened repeatedly that I overlooked this point and made excessive demands on him. Fortunately I had Major Jaich at my side to interfere at the right moment and prevent me from making grave mistakes. I had to take Jodo into a walk, pat him and talk to him until he had calmed down. When he was quiet I was allowed to begin again very carefully with the exercises. The right advice at the right moment is of invaluable help but can be given only by an instructor who has learned by practical experience to adjust work appropriately to the degree of training.

However quickly I succeeded in calming Jodo when I conscientiously followed Major Jaich's advice, I had great difficulties in regulating his paces. At the trot he had a tendency to take hasty steps. In the beginning it was impossible to ride an extended trot, which is an increase in speed by taking longer steps and by no means faster ones. My instructor employed a method that led to success in this case but that was not suitable for every horse, as I found out later. He ordered me to push Jodo forward at the rising trot until he finally took longer steps and then to reward him by a period of rest at the walk. Gradually this method proved effective with Jodo and at the end of his training he was able to perform a very brilliant extended trot. But I did not obtain the same result with other horses, especially not with those with a high knee action, such as the Lipizzaners. When pushed forward energetically, they went faster but also were more and more hasty in their steps. They became nervous and excited and lost the regularity of their paces altogether. When talking about the Lipizzaners I will explain this phenomenon.

Having worked through the winter, Jodo and I entered several competitions and right from the beginning were first or at least among the first, which was rather remarkable inasmuch as these were my first dressage tests on a horse that, apart from my short episode with Napoleon five years ago, I had trained entirely on my own. During that year of 1930 I was successful in all the horse shows in dressage tests as well as in jumping competitions—until a fall laid me up for many months.

I had to take a young thoroughbred mare over a course for the first time and she was so excited about this new experience that she rushed like mad up to a fence that had a bar across the top. She did not jump high enough and the bar got caught between her front legs and we both rolled on the ground. The fall itself would have been nothing serious but when we both had scrambled back on our feet she kicked out with both hind legs—out of fear or anger, I never knew—and hit me in the back. I went down as though struck by a lightning, was unable to get up, and was carried out of the arena with a crack in my spine. It was a very painful injury and took a long time to heal, but there was also a positive side to it. When at last, after having been partly paralysed, I was able to ride again, I had to give up jumping altogether because I could not lean forward. So I concentrated on dressage riding with all my zeal and ambition, although in the beginning I had to be lifted into the saddle.

Three years later I rode school horses again when I was posted as a student to the Spanish Riding School. And there for two years I had the privilege of learning from the Lipizzaner stallions. The Spanish Riding School is the oldest riding academy in the world. Its existence may be traced back as far as 1565.

Formerly a property of the imperial court it was taken under the control of the Department of Agriculture after the fall of the Austro-Hungarian monarchy in 1918 and continued its work of cultivating the classical art of riding. Every year the best officer of the Cavalry School was sent to the Spanish Riding School for about six or twelve months of more advanced training.

In these Lipizzaners I encountered extremely intelligent and powerful teachers who registered the smallest fault in seat or guidance and were forever ready to take advantage of their students. This "dangerous" intelligence was compensated for by the immediate advice of the riding instructors. In the daily lessons each of the three head riders dealt with a single pupil at a time, who rode a stallion that the instructor himself had trained and ridden, and with whose character and strong and weak points he was thoroughly familiar. Consequently he was able to give the appropriate order the very moment it was needed. This is certainly the most ideal method of instruction for a rider.

Up to my appointment to the Spanish Riding School my lessons had taken place in groups—one might call them classes. The instructor had to teach eight to twelve riders at a session. There were several possibilities for organizing these lessons. The instructor could take all pupils at the same time, which more or less restricted the lesson to commanding the paces and exercises and allowed only very brief corrections of the single rider. In most such cases the lesson was hard more than a shouting of "Trot!" or "Walk!" and the possibility of learning was also very limited because each student had to pay attention to the other riders. The horse as a teacher hardly came into the picture even if he possessed the capacity. An alternative was that the instructor took on one pupil after another, correcting the worst faults of the rest who worked on their own in the meantime. If he was fair and just and wanted to give each rider the privilege of this private instruction, there were not more than five to seven minutes to give to each, a span of time far too short for even the best teacher. This was in theory. In actual practice most of the instructors concentrated on a few favourite students and did not pay too much attention to the rest.

What a difference there was in the detailed and thorough instruction at the Spanish Riding School! Each of the school stallions had a personality of his own, which was marked by the personality of his rider, who had formed his individual character. The basis of the training was the same for all of them and yet the personal touch was unmistakable. Every four weeks I had a new school horse and a new instructor and I had to adapt myself to this change. The slightest difference in the training also had a repercussion on the training of the other dressage horses which I rode in the afternoon in the Prater, a large natural park on the outskirts of Vienna. Usually they took a few days to adjust themselves to the different nuances of the aids.

Riding master Polak was a great pedagogical talent, as just in giving reprimands as in giving praise. He expressed his commands in precise form and knew how to encourage the rider and give him confidence. His horses, too, went in much the same way. They were light and steady in contact and followed the slightest command. Temperamentally they were as easy and cheerful as their trainer, who was a great music lover and played the violin excellently.

Head rider Zrust had great instinctive knowledge about his horses. He was very calm with his students and followed the rule that what cannot be obtained now will succeed without effort some other day. Instead of criticising he preferred to say something agreeable, and when a pupil could not cope at all with a stallion, he mounted him himself and by the influence of his seat and legs solved the hardest problems without difficulty. His horses, however, were not as easy to ride as those of Polak and were also more difficult in temperament. They demanded an extremely quiet seat and a well-balanced application of the aids of reins and legs. But when they went well they conveyed a wonderful feeling to the rider.

Head rider Lindenbauer was an industrious man and very serious about life in general and riding in particular. He was not satisfied with himself very often and therefore did not believe in expressing any approval. The student heard hardly anything but criticisms until he succeeded with his exercises, which usually took several lessons and sometimes made him feel quite discouraged. Lindenbauer's horses went in a similarly severe manner: they demanded a correct seat, strong aids of the legs, and a firm contact with the bit. They were more work to ride inasmuch as they gave nothing without being obliged to do so, which corresponded exactly to the outlook on life of their master.

It is to the credit of the three great head riders that they preserved the standard of classical riding at the Spanish Riding School even after the breakdown of the Austro-Hungarian Empire. They continued the tradition that had been handed down through generations and they did not merely talk about it but lived it. They proved it true that the character of the rider forms his horse both physically and mentally. Under their wonderful tuition the stallions themselves grew into great teachers who helped to spread the fame of the time-honoured Riding School. From all over—from Sweden, Hungary, Germany, Switzerland, Denmark, and even Mexico—officers came to the School to learn the classical art of riding.

My first instructor was riding master Polak, who in my eyes was the best rider and unsurpassed as a teacher. My first school horse was Pluto Kerka, who reminded me immediately and unmistakably that the reins were for the horse to be guided and not for the rider to hold on to. When my contact grew too strong he leaned on the rein with all his weight or he rushed off. He could not have demonstrated more clearly how important it is to have an independent seat. But when I was able to accomplish the giving and taking action of the reins, sitting upright and bracing my back, Pluto Kerka would move with enormous impulsion and give his rider the completely new feeling of controlled power. This wonderful feeling was lost the moment the legs did not remind Pluto Kerka that the horse will move in full balance only when the hind legs carry a sufficient proportion of the weight of both horse and rider. In this respect there was much to be learned from Pluto Kerka that, as I have mentioned before, was of great help also when hunting.

Speaking about the feeling that Pluto Kerka gave me, it was by no means as I described it right from the beginning. When I rode him for the first time he surprised me by his smooth but at the same time extremely powerful movements, which I had not yet experienced with any horse. Riding without stirrups, my seat, I admit, ran into trouble, especially because the stallion was rather small and my legs are very long. When I shifted my weight about trying to regain my seat, I irritated Pluto Kerka and immediately received the message in the change of his movements. When I tried to reestablish my balance, he struck off into the canter instead of continuing his regular trot, or worse, he moved in a passage-like hovering trot that disconcerted me even more. I almost had the impression that I was on a horse for the first time in my life. I felt completely at the mercy of this ardent Lipizzaner stallion and I would never have thought that this could happen to me after all those years of riding experience. The wise old truth that with riding there is never an end of learning did not help much in this situation.

Riding master Polak, however, knew how to comfort his pupil: "Don't worry, Captain. This has happened to every new rider here!" and began to correct my seat. I had to lower my heels and sit deeper and heavier into the saddle until my weight was distributed equally on both seat bones with my spine vertical to the center of the saddle. This is how he helped me to find my balance and with Pluto Kerka calming down at once I regained my mental balance, too. Now the stallion knew what I expected from him and was no longer disturbed by my uneasy seat.

The most important thing I learned in these first lessons at the Spanish Riding School was that it does not count so much "what" is done as "how" it is done. As in any other sport, in riding it does not matter what kind of exercise the horse is executing but in what manner he performs it. But soon it dawned upon me that the correct "how" is the most difficult thing on earth. On Pluto Kerka I had to learn all over again how to break into a trot or strike off into the canter. But this time with the correct aids of seat and legs, which means that the onlooker has the impression that the rider is thinking and that the horse is executing his thought after an imperceptible communication. How difficult it is to fulfill this simple demand was proved in those first lessons with my two new masters.

Polak severely controlled my seat in all transitions and Pluto Kerka did not strike off into a canter, for instance, before he had approved of my aids and found them correct. And so it happened that in spite of years of experience on horseback I was sometimes incapable of striking off into a canter! Either I allowed the stallion to become too fast at the trot which preceded the canter, or I applied the reins too firmly and he happily offered a passage. I admit that I often felt completely ignorant and like a beginner but then on some other occasion I heard Polak's "Very good!" and picked up courage again. Maybe I was not as incapable as I sometimes felt. Gradually Polak's words of praise came more and more frequently and my despair decreased in the same measure. I was proud and pleased when after a few weeks I was able to take Pluto Kerka correctly through the corners, to execute well-rounded voltes and other exercises, and to achieve smooth transitions of paces and speed.

Perhaps it sounds strange to speak about a round volte since a volte is a small circle of six yards diameter and every circle is supposed to be round. Although a circle is supposed to be round, a volte is not always that way, as is often proved in dressage tests. In a correct volte the horse is bent in his whole body according to the circle and the inside hind leg should step under the center of gravity and therefore be bent more than the other legs, which demands a greater effort. If I did not apply Pluto Kerka's outside rein sufficiently, he turned his head too much to the inside, and if in addition, my outside leg did not hold him on the track, his hind legs would not step into the hoof prints of the forelegs. Consequently his hindquarters swung to the outside and soon there was no longer a round volte but a many-sided figure. These voltes caused more headaches to us pupils than the later execution of the most difficult exercises, which we were to learn comparatively quickly on the foundation of this minutely detailed basic training.

When I was able to perform these simple exercises according to the demands of classical riding and to the satisfaction of my instructor, Polak gradually increased the degree of difficulty. Finally, as a reward at the end of the lesson I was allowed to ride a passage on Pluto Kerka. Passage is a solemn and impressive movement which may be compared to a trot in slow motion. In the beginning, Polak with his whip supported my leg aids, which are particularly important in this pace, for the passage is dependent on the lively activity of the horse's hindquarters. Later I had to rely solely on my own aids when I wanted to enjoy having my stallion float weightlessly above the ground. The Lipizzaner has a special talent for the passage. If he is correctly trained he cannot be equalled by any other horse in this brilliant and expressive pace. Maybe this is the reason why at the Spanish Riding School the passage is called the "Spanish step"!

Lipizzaners may be very cunning, too, if they find out how to make life easier for themselves. There was the stallion named Maestoso Borina, who reached the unheard-of age of thirty-three years and whom I kept in retirement in the stables when I had become Director of the School. Under his master, the head rider Zrust, he was able to show a very brilliant passage, but one day when he was being ridden by an elderly civilian student, I saw him perform a rather strange movement which with some imagination might have been taken for a passage. Lifting his front legs high and slowly as for a passage, he followed with his hind legs at a comfortable walk, swinging his back in such a way that his rider bobbed up and down in the saddle. When I pointed out this extraordinary sight to head rider Zrust he winked at me and smiled: "Just leave him alone! Why shouldn't he? The old gentleman is happy because he thinks he is riding a perfect passage—and the stallion does not tire himself out!"

Polak's favourite was Favory Montenegra, to whom I owe a great deal. He was a gorgeous stallion, very graceful and remarkably intelligent. Under his master he was capable of performing piaffe and passage with a perfection I was absolutely unable to achieve. Either my seat disturbed his balance, to which he reacted immediately with less elevated steps, or I applied the reins too strongly so that his hind legs were pushing more than carrying the weight and the movement was no longer floating. Often I was in despair of ever reaching perfection, but then for the fraction of a second I felt how the stallion became higher in front and as light as a feather before this extraordinary sensation was lost again. When I succeeded in controlling my seat and guiding the stallion with ever lighter contact, these moments were more and more frequent until Favory Montenegra effortlessly floated above the ground in a piaffe and passage of such brilliance that the spectators at the morning training broke into spontaneous applause although this was not at all "done" in those days. When Polak nodded "beautiful" in my direction I felt royally rewarded. Forever will I be grateful to these two great masters.

Most of my lessons with head rider Zrust were on Conversano Nobila. I was allowed to ride him even though he went under his master in the Sunday performance. As he gave me quite a bit of trouble I learned from him how to ride the more difficult horses. But when I succeeded in making him understand what I wanted, he gave me the wonderful feeling of a passage full of impulsion. Presently I found out that there was a difference between his passage and that of Pluto Kerka. Pluto Kerka bent his forelegs in the front knee and lifted his forearm until it was horizontal to the ground before putting it down in a beautifully round motion which gained little ground to the front. Conversano Nobila lifted his legs in the same way but stretched them out more before putting them down in a longer and more forward action. I was told that the first kind is called the "round" passage and the second kind the "long" one. Later I found out that horses with a high knee action have greater ability for the "round" passage but that in the extended trot their legs do not reach forward to a very great extent. Those that are capable of a brilliant extension in the trot tend to perform a "long" passage, which is what we see with most dressage horses since they are generally half- and Thoroughbreds and very seldom Lipizzaners.

This description should not, however, give the impression that I was riding the paces of the high school, among which we count the passage, right from the beginning of my lessons with head rider Zrust. On the contrary, it took a long time to obtain this privilege because at first I had great difficulties with Conversano Nobila. I was unable to collect him because he was inclined to go above the bit. Lifting his head and losing contact with the bit, he dropped his back and by this attitude made it impossible to execute any exercise correctly. Zrust had infinite patience with me and I was intent on following his example. I pushed Conversano Nobila carefully forward with both legs and tried to absorb the impulsion with my braced back and the reins well applied. He was supposed not to increase his speed but with a beautifully shaped neck become short in his whole body—collected is the technical term.

Finally I succeeded in achieving this form when riding on the large circle, and was able to begin work on the track in the whole arena, trying to maintain this collection when performing various exercises. If I lost it again I had to return to the large circle, where it is easier to obtain collection because of the increased bend of the horse's inside hind leg. Thus I realised the meaning of collection, which might be compared to the mental concentration of a human being. If the collection was assured, if Conversano Nobila accepted the bit in the correct attitude and position of head and neck and his hind legs stepped sufficiently under his body, then even the most difficult exercises succeeded without apparent effort. If I did not obtain the correct collection, horse and rider were covered with sweat without obtaining a satisfactory result. This proves how important it is to prepare the horse correctly and how much of the daily work should be devoted to this preparation. It consists of the correct execution of the simple exercises such as straightening, loosening, and relaxing the horse, physically and mentally, until he is concentrating completely on his rider. At this point the rider may collect his horse and then even the most difficult airs of the high school seem easy as play. Conversano Nobila was the first Lipizzaner I rode after being appointed Director of the Spanish Riding School in 1939, thus renewing an old friendship.

It was a special mark of distinction when head rider Zrust entrusted his favourite horse, Conversano Savona, to my care. In the performances he presented this beautiful stallion in the levade in the pillars and in hand and sometimes in the most superb manner under the rider. For many years Conversano Savona had been the best in levades. In the lesson he had to be led with very delicate aids and not disturbed by any awkwardness for he was full of temperament, which he preserved until his old age. If Conversano Savona worked especially well with me, I felt very happy and his master also beamed. As a reward I was allowed to perform a levade with this wonderful Lipizzaner.

In the levade the horse rises on his lowered hocks with his forelegs tucked under him and remains motionless for a few seconds in this position. Many equestrian monuments depict horse and rider in this attitude—for instance, that of Prince Eugene of Savoy which stands on the Heldenplatz in Vienna. In bygone days the airs above the ground, that is, exercises in which the horse lifts his forelegs or both fore- and hind legs off the ground, belonged to the training of every school horse and every rider. They may be seen on many old etchings and paintings. Today they are preserved in their living form only at the Spanish Riding School.

The correct levade is developed from a lively piaffe in which the hind legs will step more and more under the body until the weight is finally shifted onto the hindquarters and the forehand is lifted off the ground. I had a strange feeling when Conversano Savona did his first levade with me. He lowered his hindquarters as if he was going to sit down and lifted his forelegs until his body formed an angle of forty-five degrees to the ground. I sat on an oblique basis and had to maintain unaltered the position of my body vertical to the ground. If I leaned forward ever so little Conversano Savona ended his levade. The same happened if I took my body behind the vertical line. To me he seemed like a juggler who will try to step under the center of gravity of the object he is balancing. It was yet another proof of the eminent importance of balance in any kind of equitation.

When head rider Zrust died in 1940 I took Conversano Savona under my special protection and tried to make his retirement the pleasant one he certainly deserved. In hand he showed the levade for many more years and gave pleasure to thousands of spectators from all over the world. When he died this great stallion from whom I had learned so much was twenty-nine years of age, which was the best proof of the correct training by his master. For like any other gymnastics, riding should strengthen the horse and prolong his life.

With head rider Lindenbauer it was chiefly Pluto Austria that I had to ride in the lessons. This stallion demanded that the aids be given in a particularly strong manner. Besides he had an inclination to go above the rein. He carried his head high and paid more attention to what was going on around him than he did to his rider. Because he raised his head and neck too high he dropped his back and consequently could not step sufficiently under his body with his hind legs. If this was the case his movements became very uncomfortable, so rough and difficult to sit that I bumped clumsily on his back. The more heavily his rider hit the saddle the higher he raised his head and neck and the more he dropped his back. It was by no means a pleasure to ride him, especially not with the criticisms of the instructor as a musical background. Once dismounting after such a lesson without any tangible result and having saluted head rider Lindenbauer according to the tradition of the School, I sighed in complete dejection. "I think I better give up riding altogether," I said. "I am never going to learn it!"

Lindenbauer was all the more vexed by this remark. "Nonsense, Captain, you should have more confidence in yourself!"

This put the lid on my discouragement and I replied: "Even if I had had confidence in myself this lesson today would have shattered it completely. But it's my nature that I am hardly ever content with myself!" Smiling at last, Lindenbauer shook my hand and said that he could understand me so well because he, too, was always so strict with himself.

At long last I succeeded in riding Pluto Austria energetically forward and by repeated short actions of the reins made him accept the bit with a lowered head and a long neck until he arched his back and his hind legs were able to step sufficiently under the body. This made the correct collection possible and I could sit comfortably and with a good feeling at last.

There was another school horse who gave me some trouble. His name was Maestoso Africa and not Maestoso Austria. The reason I mention this is because a book was published with the title *Maestoso Austria* when I was Director of the School and many visitors came to see this famous stallion. They were very disappointed when all I could show them was either Maestoso Africa or Pluto Austria. A stallion with the name of Maestoso Austria has never existed at the Spanish Riding School.

Maestoso Africa was a problem for me to ride because he was very small and I had great trouble placing my long legs and putting my knees in the correct spot. Since the aids of my legs could not be fully employed I was reduced to giving the aids mainly with the weight of my body. This was quite difficult in the beginning but helped to establish an independent seat. After a while Maestoso Africa and I got well on together and I was very pleased when head rider Zrust asked me one day teasingly whether I would not want to be transferred to the Spanish Riding School and employed as a rider since I rode Maestoso Africa better and especially in a more brilliant passage than his own rider. Although said as a joke this remark was a sign of esteem which any instructor should express to his pupil at the right moment. When I was an instructor myself I followed this example whenever appropriate praise was justified.

During the two years in which I was stationed at the Spanish Riding School as a student I had the opportunity of studying the characters of both horses and riders and, in the twenty-six years during which I was responsible for the School as director, I enlarged my knowledge considerably. Just as human professors develop into real characters in the course of their long lives, so did the four-legged teachers who all year round had to submit in obedience to their trainers and also to endure the awkwardness and clumsiness of the students. It was certainly no pleasure to have to begin all over again with each new pupil, forever feeling the wrong kinds of aids and suffering an incorrect seat that irritated the balance. But because they were personalities they found out how to take it easy or to play tricks on their riders, as did Generale Malaga, a school stallion who had been trained by head rider Zrust.

Generale Malaga's specialty was pirouettes. With great skill and perfection he performed this exercise, which is the smallest turn at the canter. Once there was a dressage rider, a lieutenant colonel who had encountered difficulties when he wanted to teach these pirouettes to his dressage horse. He came to head rider Zrust for a few lessons in order to learn the correct feeling of this exercise. He was a very good-looking officer and quite arrogant. He brought his wife to the School so that she would be able to see how well he would execute the pirouettes right at the first attempt. He mounted Generale Malaga and began to limber him up, disregarding Zrust's corrective remark that he should not take his upper body so much forward. He replied simply that he was used to riding like this and that the position of the upper part was a matter of taste and varied according to the individual. Zrust shook his head and pointed out that the stallion was accustomed to the rider sitting in the manner traditional with the classical art of riding, and that he was unable to feel the aids of the seat of the rider leaned forward. The lieutenant colonel shrugged and retorted: "He will have to get accustomed to it. After all, I am the boss!" Zrust lifted his shoulders as was his habit and said that Generale Malaga was sufficiently warmed up and the officer might begin the pirouettes now.

Full of enthusiasm the lieutenant colonel followed the suggestion. He paid hardly any attention to the commands of Zrust and rode as near as possible to where his wife sat so that she would be able to admire his beautiful pirouette at close range. Generale Malaga, however, obviously thought that it was too much to insist on pirouettes without exercising the appropriate influence with the correct seat. In the middle of the turn he performed a tremendous leap and the rider sailed through the air. Zrust winked an eye towards me: "A hair's breadth and Mandi [this was what he called the stallion] would have landed him in his wife's lap. Why didn't he believe me when I told him that he should sit more upright?"

By the way, the stallions were not at all impressed by any kind of uniform. They unseated the lieutenant colonel in mufti just as readily as the major in uniform even if he came from across the ocean. The Mexican Major Rodriguez was stationed at the Spanish Riding School for two years and later was for many years the teacher of the famous and successful Mexican jumping rider General Mariles. He, too, was deposited in the sand, by Maestoso Sardinia, after a short altercation, but got on his legs with the agility of a cat, bent down, and said to his instructor with a smile that he had wanted to pick up his whip which he had dropped. Thus he saved his face and avoided paying the usual fine of ten pounds of sugar. The instructor did not dare to contradict the foreign officer.

We have already talked about the cunning Maestoso Borina. He did not limit his tricks to the arena but expressed his personality at every occasion. When he was advanced in age he was included among the happy few who appeared in the floodlights of the Vienna State Opera. In the Opera *The Girl of the Golden West,* to the melodies of Puccini, he had to carry the famous singer Maria Jeritza onto the stage. She was an accomplished rider, and he made an excellent appearance as he entered with graceful steps and stood like a monument while the artist sang her aria. It was a most impressive scene, and Maestoso Borina seemed thoroughly to enjoy the special applause he received. Soon he knew his part so well that he was not to be held backstage and pushed ahead when the music for his scene began. One day there was a rolled-up carpet in his way. Madame Jeritza, very excited, demanded that this obstacle be removed, and in that moment the music set in. There was no holding Maestoso Borina. With determination he cleared the obstacle, much to the dismay of the lady on his back, and precisely on time, he appeared before the public, which greeted him with applause while his rider tried to recover breath for her song.

Having grown old and wise, Neapolitano Montenuova ranked among those conscientious creatures who take their work very seriously and know exactly what they want. This stallion had been trained by head rider Lindenbauer, who tenderly called him Peppi, which in Vienna is short for Joseph. He had enhanced the school performances by his great abilities and the beauty of his movements for more than twenty years. In his old days—he reached the age of thirty-one years—his task was to examine the candidates for careers as riders at the Spanish Riding School who, until 1944, came from the Army. While willingly following the commands of good riders and executing all exercises with his habitual submission, he found out the weak ones with incredible instinct and embarrassed many a rider who took himself for a great artist.

There was another of these characters who helped him as a co-judge. Pluto Siglavy had formerly performed caprioles and his trainer Polak had called him Schatzl, which means "little treasure." Having reached the age of twenty-two years, he no longer appeared in the performances but continued to serve as a school horse. He was more severe than Neapolitano Montenuova and when he encountered a clumsy rider he wasted little patience on him. With a tremendous capriole he set an end to this unpleasant experience and landed the all-too-hopeful candidate in the sand.

On one occasion I was confronted with a difficult situation. I had to choose one candidate from two young riders of approximately equal qualifications. Together Neapolitano Montenuova and Pluto Siglavy were brought into the arena. Both rides mounted at the same time and rode in accordance with my commands, which gave me the opportunity to compare their abilities. Again they seemed quite equal and the decision was really hard to make. All of a sudden Pluto Siglavy came to my rescue and spilled his rider. I was glad to have support for my decision, but in order to be absolutely just, I had the riders change horses. What followed now was totally unexpected. Maybe Pluto Siglavy was annoyed by this additional work and, remembering the pleasure and relief of a capriole, after a few minutes landed the second candidate in the sand, too. Thus he evaded his responsibility and left the difficult decision entirely to me.

Oh, those school stallions—there is no end to stories and anecdotes about them. I have certainly learned to respect their personalities and to acknowledge them as teachers. On the other hand they become teachers only when the rider endeavours to understand their reactions and their behaviour. Since they cannot speak they are limited to signals. Perhaps many a rider may even be called lucky that they are unable to speak because they would often have occasion to put in complaints about incomprehension, ignorance, impatience, injustice, and ingratitude. Instead they serve man in silent and irrevocable loyalty.

From Sailboats to Snaffles
in One Easy Marriage

From *Horsefolk Are Different*

BY COOKY McCLUNG

Cooky McClung has been called, and with good reason, "the Erma Bombeck of the horsy set." Her columns in *The Chronicle of the Horse* are one of the first things that subscribers turn to. And as anyone who knows Cooky is well aware, she's just as entertaining in person as she is in print.

⊰◈⊱

Before he met her, the man spent his leisure time sailing. On weekends or long evenings he'd simply hop in the boat, cast off and up the mainsail, tacking to and fro among the whitecaps. Before he met her his life had order and regimentation and schedules he could stick with. He had a house with a yard and a toolshed.

But she had horses. He met her and fell in love and married her, and part of the wedding vows were "love me, love my horses." It was part and parcel of the whole relationship.

The order and regimen in his life floated across the horizon with most of his friends sailing off to leave him while he spent his weekends going to horse shows. Her schedules became his schedules, if you could call them that, which he never did because they varied from week to week and even day to day. The only constant in this new world of variables was that the horses were always fed on time.

He pondered the fact that, unlike the horses that were now a part of his life, his boat only ate when he used it. It did, of course, need gasoline in the tank to get him home should the wind happen to die down to nothing. His new bride pointed out, ever so subtly of course, that horses did not need to rely on anything so fickle as a puff of wind to move along.

Because the house with the yard and toolshed was in no way sufficient to keep several big, strong horses, the couple sold the man's house and went in search of a farm. To be fair, she looked very hard for a farm somewhat near a body of water where her spouse could still enjoy his beloved boat.

They compromised finally, and found a lovely house with a large pasture, two fine paddocks and a barn just 200 feet from their dwelling. They moved the boat to a cove 26 miles and two toll bridges away. If the man noticed a slight inequity in the fact that she could merely throw on a jacket over her pajamas and hop down to feed the horses, while he had to shave and pack a lunch to visit his boat, he was courteous enough not to mention it.

Although he was a fair enough handyman, tinkering about with his boat to keep the cogs and wheels and pulleys working, he had never had much experience keeping a farm in order. The boat had a large anchor that plunked into the water and a heavy rope on the bow that secured it to the dock where the boat obediently stayed until he wanted to use it. The man learned rather quickly that horses needed more elaborate forms of restraint and even if tied they often became disobedient.

The stable itself was in pretty good repair, and the man found little to do other than to fix the odd latch, fill in some holes in the stall floors and clear out a few months' accumulation of cobwebs and dirt. Neighbors visited often, and the man grew more familiar with horse terminology. When early on, one suggested he put a loafing shed in the big pasture, the man said, "That sounds nice; what's a loafing shed?"

The neighbors showed him what a loafing shed was, and that they could be built in different sizes, depending on how many horses wanted to stand under it (without fighting for space) in a thunderstorm. The man had never worried too much about his boat being out in a thunderstorm, even if it included lightning. Lightning was a consideration with horses wearing iron shoes, and did not bounce off them as harmlessly as it might a boat's mast.

And of course he had to install water troughs in the pasture and the paddocks, with no-freeze lines running to them. In the winter, when water froze, the boat was lifted out of its habitat and put into storage until the spring thaw. Horses, the man's bride pointed out again, were quite usable all year 'round. Even if one put them in storage, however, they still needed to eat.

The man also discovered that, while boats had a great number of accoutrements, horses had more. Naturally, the horses had come with quite an extensive wardrobe of tack and sheets and blankets and saddle pads and bandages and galloping boots. But it seemed something was always wearing out or being outgrown, something always needed breaking in, sewing up or soaping down. Once, when the man's wife was away for an afternoon, he decided to surprise her by washing four dirty turn-out blankets in their new washing machine. The Maytag repairman had something to do the next day.

And then, of course, there was the actual riding part. The man soon realized that if he wanted to spend more time with his new wife, he'd better learn how to actually get on and steer a horse. He envisioned cantering over the lovely countryside together, romantically picturing the television ad of horses moving gracefully along in slow motion as the couple smiled lovingly at each other. Reality was somewhat different.

While there was more to do to get a boat underway, once abroad with all the sails in place, one had only to stretch out on the deck and more or less guide the sail to determine the boat's direction. Because he was an intelligent man, it took him only a few seconds to discover that, even in a ring where he started to ride, if he just sat limply on a horse and barely held the reins, the direction the horse would choose would very likely not be the one of the man's choice. The horse would choose to simply drop his head and eat grass, thus allowing the man to slide unceremoniously down his neck, or would head for the barn and wait for dinner.

One had to be more in command, so to speak, upon a horse than on a boat deck. There was no first mate to give orders to if the horse happened to drift in the wrong direction. Also, the man pointed out after having done it several times, if he fell off a horse it hurt a lot more hitting the ground than if he fell off the boat and hit the water. Also, nine times out of 10, the horse would not wait for him to get back aboard. Neither, insisted his bride, would a boat, only a horse didn't go all the way to England if turned loose.

Because the man loved his wife dearly, he persevered. He traded his docksiders in for field boots, his cutoffs for breeches and his sweatshirt for a well-tailored hacking jacket. And he practiced every day, after work on long spring and summer evenings and every weekend, riding around the ring until he mastered posting to the trot and sitting to the canter, and gained enough experience to go across country.

They had searched and searched to find the man a horse with a personality like his boat's, a horse that did pretty much what you told it to do. His wife's horses, while tractable enough with an experienced rider, took advantage of a novice, and the man often longed for an anchor to "throw overboard" when they got going a little too fast.

Actually, the turning point in the man's formerly tidy, well-balanced life came when he got his very own horse. Even his den metamorphosed from a place with framed pictures of whaling vessels and artifacts of nautical persuasion, to one with blue and red ribbons and pedigrees of fine Thoroughbred lineage on the wall and bridles hanging over the back of his easy chair.

Not unlike a new parent, he took an avid interest in his own horse, fussing and pampering. While he had once secretly thought that, unlike sailing, riding was a pastime invented so that people could avoid work, now it became his avocation. He found himself making trips to the tack shop to buy articles he had formerly been unable to spell, and at dinner parties he began to take an active aprt in horsy discussions.

He even considered canceling his vacation plans. No one would take care of his horse the way he could. He was not concerned any more about his house. The house could burn to the ground. But he worried terribly that the horse would not be fed properly or that it might hurt itself and whoever was left in charge might not notice.

Some evenings his wife would find him just sitting in the pasture among the daisies like Ferdinand among his flowers, watching his very own horse as it strolled about chomping grass. The man entered small, local horse show classes, bringing home ribbons in such things as adult equitation and low hunter to add to the den wall collection. The following fall he was introduced to foxhunting, and thus began the demise of the man's boating interest.

His wife suggested that the man could still sail in the summertime and hunt in the fall and winter and go to some shows in the spring. But, of course, the horse might lose condition, and there was so much to do.

The man could be found forever revarnishing the stall doors, mowing the pasture, cleaning tack and displaying it on the new racks he'd built, or even mucking out. Mucking out, the man insisted, was good exercise and gave one time to contemplate the good things in life.

Finally they took one last trip to the cove to visit the boat, sitting forlornly in the water with cobwebs on the mast. "I suppose," said the man thoughtfully, "that it's time to sell the boat to someone who will really enjoy it." Watching it bob about on the mooring, he added, "I loved that boat a lot, but in all the years I had it, it never loved me back."

The Diverting History of John Gilpin

BY WILLIAM COWPER

William Cowper (1731–1800) was an eighteenth century pre-Romantic poet and essayist who is best known for religious writing. "The Diverting History of John Gilpin" is a rollicking account of what happened when the subject's horse overshot the destination not once but twice (it reminds me of the line about not wanting a horse that goes in a snaffle but one that *stops* in a snaffle).

John Gilpin was a citizen
  Of credit and renown,
A train-band Captain eke was he
  Of famous London town.

John Gilpin's spouse said to her dear,
  "Though wedded we have been
These twice ten tedious years, yet we
  No holiday have seen.

To-morrow is our wedding day,
  And we will then repair
Unto the Bell at Edmonton,
  All in a chaise and pair.

My sister and my sister's child,
  Myself and children three,
Will fill the chaise, so you must ride
  On horseback after we."

He soon replied,—"I do admire
   Of womankind but one,
And you are she, my dearest dear,
   Therefore it shall be done.

I am a linen-draper bold,
   As all the world doth know,
And my good friend the Calender
   Will lend his horse to go."

Quoth Mrs. Gilpin,—"That's well said,
   And for that wine is dear,
We will be furnish'd with our own,
   Which is both bright and clear."

John Gilpin kiss'd his loving wife;
   O'erjoyed was he to find
That though on pleasure she was bent,
   She had a frugal mind.

The morning came, the chaise was brought,
   But yet was not allow'd
To drive up to the door, lest all
   Should say that she was proud.

So three doors off the chaise was stay'd,
   Where they did all get in;
Six precious souls, and all agog
   To dash through thick and thin.

Smack went the whip, round went the wheels,
   Were never folk so glad,
The stones did rattle underneath
   As if Cheapside were mad.

John Gilpin at his horse's side,
   Seized fast the flowing mane,
And up he got, in haste to ride,
   But soon came down again;

For saddle-tree scarce reach'd had he,
   His journey to begin,
When, turning round his head, he saw
   Three customers come in.

So down he came; for loss of time,
   Although it grieved him sore,
Yet loss of pence, full well he knew,
   Would trouble him much more.

'T was long before the customers
   Were suited to their mind,
When Betty screaming, came downstairs,
   "The wine is left behind!"

"Good lack!" quoth he, "yet bring it me,
   My leathern belt likewise,
In which I bear my trusty sword
   When I do exercise."

Now mistress Gilpin, careful soul!
   Had two stone bottles found,
To hold the liquor that she loved,
   And keep it safe and sound.

Each bottle had a curling ear,
   Through which the belt he drew,
And hung a bottle on each side,
   To make his balance true.

Then over all, that he might be
   Equipp'd from top to toe,
His long red cloak, well brush'd and neat,
   He manfully did throw.

Now see him mounted once again
   Upon his nimble steed,
Full slowly pacing o'er the stones
   With caution and good heed.

But, finding soon a smoother road
 Beneath his well-shod feet,
The snorting beast began to trot,
 Which gall'd him in his seat,

So "Fair and softly," John he cried,
 But John he cried in vain;
That trot became a gallop soon,
 In spite of curb and rein.

So stooping down, as needs he must
 Who cannot sit upright,
He grasp'd the mane with both his hands,
 And eke with all his might.

His horse, who never in that sort
 Had handled been before,
What thing upon his back had got
 Did wonder more and more.

Away went Gilpin, neck or nought,
 Away went hat and wig!
He little dreamt when he set out
 Of running such a rig!

The wind did blow, the cloak did fly,
 Like streamer long and gay,
Till, loop and button failing both,
 At last it flew away.

Then might all people well discern
 The bottles he had slung;
A bottle swinging at each side,
 As hath been said or sung.

The dogs did bark, the children scream'd,
 Up flew the windows all,
And ev'ry soul cried out, "Well done!"
 As loud as he could bawl.

Away went Gilpin—who but he?
  His fame soon spread around—
"He carries weight!" "He rides a race!"
  "'T is for a thousand pound!"

And still, as fast as he drew near,
  'T was wonderful to view,
How in a trice the turnpike-men
  Their gates wide open threw.

And now, as he went bowing down
  His reeking head full low,
The bottles twain behind his back
  Were shattered at a blow.

Down ran the wine into the road,
  Most piteous to be seen,
Which made his horse's flanks to smoke
  As they had basted been.

But still he seem'd to carry weight,
  With leathern girdle braced,
For all might see the bottle-necks
  Still dangling at his waist.

Thus all through merry Islington
  These gambols he did play,
Until he came unto the Wash
  Of Edmonton so gay.

And there he threw the Wash about
  On both sides of the way,
Just like unto a trundling mop,
  Or a wild-goose at play.

At Edmonton his loving wife
  From the balcony spied
Her tender husband, wond'ring much
  To see how he did ride.

"Stop, stop, John Gilpin!—Here's the house!"
   They all at once did cry;
"The dinner waits and we are tired:"
   Said Gilpin—"So am I!"

But yet his horse was not a whit
   Inclined to tarry there;
For why?—his owner had a house
   Full ten miles off, at Ware,

So like an arrow swift he flew,
   Shot by an archer strong;
So did he fly—which brings me to
   The middle of my song.

Away went Gilpin, out of breath,
   And sore against his will,
Till at his friend the Calender's
   His horse at last stood still.

The Calender, amazed to see
   His neighbour in such trim,
Laid down his pipe, flew to the gate,
   And thus accosted him:—

"What news? what news? your tidings tell,
   Tell me you must and shall—
Say why bare-headed you are come,
   Or why you come at all?"

Now Gilpin had a pleasant wit,
   And loved a timely joke,
And thus unto the Calender
   In merry guise he spoke:—

"I came because your horse would come;
   And if I well forebode,
My hat and wig will soon be here,
   They are upon the road."

The Calender, right glad to find
   His friend in merry pin,
Return'd him not a single word,
   But to the house went in;

Whence straight he came with hat and wig,
   A wig that flow'd behind,
A hat not much the worse for wear,
   Each comely in its kind.

He held them up, and in his turn
   Thus show'd his ready wit:—
"My head is twice as big as yours,
   They therefore needs must fit.

But let me scrape the dirt away
   That hangs upon your face;
And stop and eat, for well you may
   Be in a hungry case."

Said John—"It is my wedding-day,
   And all the world would stare,
If wife should dine at Edmonton,
   And I should dine at Ware."

So, turning to his horse, he said—
   "I am in haste to dine;
'T was for your pleasure you came here,
   You shall go back for mine."

Ah, luckless speech and bootless boast!
   For which he paid full dear;
For, while he spake, a braying ass
   Did sing most loud and clear;

Whereat his horse did snort, as he
   Had heard a lion roar,
And gallop'd off with all his might,
   As he had done before.

Away went Gilpin, and away
   Went Gilpin's hat and wig!
He lost them sooner than at first,
   For why?—they were too big!

Now Mistress Gilpin, when she saw
   Her husband posting down
Into the country far away,
   She pull'd out half-a-crown;

And thus unto the youth she said
   That drove them to the Bell—
"This shall be yours when you bring back
   My husband safe and well."

The youth did ride, and soon did meet
   John coming back amain;
Whom in a trice he tried to stop,
   By catching at his rein;

But not performing what he meant,
   And gladly would have done,
The frighted steed he frighted more,
   And made him faster run.

Away went Gilpin, and away
   Went post-boy at his heels!—
The post-boy's horse right glad to miss
   The lumb'ring of the wheels.

Six gentlemen upon the road,
   Thus seeing Gilpin fly,
With post-boy scramp'ring in the rear,
   They raised the hue and cry:—

"Stop thief! stop thief—a highwayman!"
   Not one of them was mute;
And all and each that pass'd that way
   Did join in the pursuit.

And now the turnpike gates again
  Flew open in short space;
The toll-men thinking, as before,
  That Gilpin rode a race.

And so he did, and won it too,
  For he got first to town;
Nor stopp'd till where he had got up
  He did again get down.

Now let us sing, Long live the king,
  And Gilpin, long live he;
And when he next doth ride abroad,
  May I be there to see!

Tip on a Lost Race

BY CAREY WINFREY

Carey Winfrey, at present an editor at *People Magazine,* is a product of Columbia College, the Marines, Columbia Graduate School of Journalism, and the racetrack. As this selection from his memoir *Starts and Finishes: Coming of Age in the Fifties* indicates, the last of these institutions may have been of the greatest educative value.

His father, Bill Winfrey, was voted into the Racing Hall of Fame in 1972.

It was only by coincidence that my father arrived the week before I did. He had come East for the yearling auctions to advise a wealthy Mexican in the art of buying horses. The previous year the Mexican paid some $100,000 for a nineteen-year-old stallion and, horse longevity being roughly one-fourth of a man's, there had been suggestions that he seek the advice of a horseman before continuing his speculations in equine bloodstock. That's what my father was doing in Saratoga.

I had seen him last in California. I drove up to the stable one morning early. When I got out of the car, the first thing my father said to me was, "You're certainly wearing your hair long."

"I guess so. The effete East, you know."

"Well, if it gets any longer," my father said, "you can stay in the East." Then he apologized. "You're grown now," he said. "You can do what you like." But he looked at the ground a lot the rest of the weekend I was there.

My father had already returned to California by the time I got to Saratoga. But it was almost as if he were still there. Everywhere I went, people told me that they'd seen him and how well he looked.

Six years ago my father set an all-time money-winning record as a trainer of thoroughbred horses. Led by two two-year-old champions (Bold Lad and Queen Empress), his stable won nearly a million and a half dollars in purse money (of which my father, as trainer, got roughly 10 per cent). Astounding to many, the next year he walked away from that same stable—easily the best in the country—citing personal reasons for his resignation. The wire services carried a blurb about Bill Winfrey "retiring" from racing at the age of fifty. He didn't retire though, and even today there is lingering speculation around the racetrack as to why he left. The only reason my father ever gave was that the job took too much time away from his family. I certainly never had any trouble believing that that was the real reason. Still, there were a lot of rumors that my father had not gotten along all that well with one of the stable's owners, Ogden Phipps, a thoroughbred breeder, member of the Jockey Club, racing official, and one of the half-dozen or so most powerful men in American racing.

I am nine or ten years old and deep asleep in the still hour before dawn. In a little while my father will come and sit on the edge of my bed, rubbing my back slow and warm to wake me. But now I am dreaming: I am watching Les or John or one of the other grooms braid the tail of a gleaming chestnut colt, beautifying him for a race. I am sitting cross-legged at the door of the stall, listening to the soft, whispering psssssssss, psssssssss music the groom makes, exhaling, to keep the horse hairs from getting in his mouth, when my father appears, upset. "The jock can't ride," he announces to no one in particular. "We'll have to scratch."

Now the dream gets a little hazy. But somehow, miraculously, there I am, splendidly annointed in racing silks, the whip in my right hand, the stirrups pulled so high my knees touch my hands. Now the dream is clear again. We are led into the starting gate. I hear my heart tharumping in my chest. "No chance, Mr. Cassidy," I yell to the starter. Then my horse is still. The bell rings, the doors fly open, and with an incredible lurch that all but throws me from the saddle, we are off. I hit the colt three times with my whip, each time in stride—bam, pause, bam, pause, bam—just to get him going. We settle back for the stretch drive and I lean back holding him in, saving his speed, rating him, riding easy. When we round the last turn and head for home, I begin to hear the roar in the grandstand. I am whipping again, now, as we pass horses on the outside, the colt and I moving as one. Now there is but one horse in front of me and, as I creep up on him it is all I can do to keep asleep for my inevitable, but still incredible . . . Victory . . . by a nose.

Maybe a jockey was the only thing I ever really wanted to be. The thought occurs to me now, walking my father's and grandfather's paths here at Saratoga. Breathing this air that is a perfume of linament, pine, oats, straw, and, yes, manure, I am once again "Bill's boy," my father's son, dependent on his praise for my solace, ready at his bidding to remount a frisky palomino that has just run off and thrown me.

We would get up those mornings about 5:30, my father and I, splashing cold water on our faces to wake us, moving quietly through the house so as not to disturb my mother. The streetlights would be haloed in the morning dew as we drove through near-deserted streets, the radio blaring Frankie Laine and "Mule Traaaaaaaiiiin . . . clippety cloppin' over hill and dale . . ." We would sing to the radio, in tune only with each other. I would lean against my father's warmth and never suspect there was any other thing to be but happy.

We'd arrive at first light, and the first set of horses, half a dozen or so, would already be saddled. The exercise boys, seeing us arrive, would put down their coffees and get ready to get aboard their horses. I would walk down the long shed past two dozen horses in their stalls. It was a ritual my father insisted on—saying good morning to the grooms and exercise boys who worked for him. "Good morning, 'Apples,' " "Good morning, Harold."

Once the riders had mounted, the exercise boys would lead the horses to the training track, while I would follow my father on foot to the clocking stand, stopping with him along the way as he exchanged cheery small talk ("You know my boy Carey") with the other trainers. The fact that I never managed to decipher it never prevented my enjoying the cryptic language of the clockers: "Twenty-two and two for the bay colt. What'ju get him in, Jack?" By the time we'd get back to the stable, the grooms would have unsaddled the horses and would have started washing them. The exercise boys, each holding the shank of their mounts, would relive the workout, speaking the present-tense vernacular of race-trackese: "Well, we break real good at the quarter pole, but then this filly she see a bird or something and she break stride . . ." The horses, sweating and frisky now, would kick out with their hind feet as the grooms ("Hey now poppa, what'sa matter with you") lavished steaming buckets of hot water on their sweating bodies, applying it in great dripping sponges before whisking them dry with long aluminum scrapers. Often, after the horses' baths, my father would let me take the shank of a quieter colt or filly and I'd join the seemingly endless oval parade around the cooling-out ring.

But the best part of the morning was when it came time to ride the pony. For as long as I could remember, my father's pony was named Bill. I don't know how many Pony Bills there were in all in the years I spent weekends and summers at the track, but I do know that I fell off just about every one of them. Even if I was hurt, as happened a couple of times, my father would always make me get right back on and ride some more.

I never suspected that such rides would mark the end of my memory's view of childhood. I didn't know that my parents would soon be divorced, or that I would be sent, in the fifth grade, to a military school in Maryland—out of range, the thinking ran, of any of the attendant acrimony. Nor could I know that I would come to look upon such mornings at the racetrack as my strongest ties to earth and place, my strongest link to the kind of heritage I would read about in the library of that school.

A dream much like mine had actually come true for my father. Twice, in fact. As a boy of nine, he won his first horse race, riding a circus pony named Sparkle, not too much bigger than he was, at the old Jamaica track on Long Island. I don't know how many other horses there were in the race, but I have been told they were under considerable restraint. In the picture taken in the winner's circle, my father's nine-year-old face is very serious, but the men standing around in black suits and hats behind him are all smiles.

When he was seventeen, he won his second race, this time in real competition. "Congratulations," says the telegram in my grandmother's scrapbook. "Bill won his first race today." It was signed by my grandfather, "Carey." Next to it, a yellowed clipping is more detailed: "Willie Winfrey rode his first winner here this afternoon. Son of G. Carey Winfrey, well-known owner and trainer, Willie has been trying to crash the winner's circle since early in the last Florida campaign. . . . Eight answered the call, but little Willie showed them the way home. He brought the B. B. Stable's two-year-old from behind in a rattling stretch drive to take command in the closing strides. The stable gang gave the little boy a great big hand."

The applause notwithstanding, my father has always said that the greatest mistake he made in life was quitting school in the ninth grade to become a jockey.

My father's riding career lasted less than a year. Having put on too much weight to continue as a jockey, he became, at eighteen, the country's youngest licensed horse trainer, taking a string of my grandfather's stable up to Canada. By the time I was born (1941, the year Whirlaway won the Triple Crown), my father had a small reputation and was developing better and better horses for a series of owners. When, in the late 1940s, Alfred G. Vanderbilt asked

him to take charge of his once-commanding stable, my father willingly ac-
cepted and the next year found himself with three stakes winners (Bed O
Roses, Next Move, and Loser Weeper); he had become one of the most talked-
about young trainers in the country. But his greatest success was yet to come.
As I cried myself to homesick sleep in a dormitory near Baltimore in 1951, at
Vanderbilt's Sagamore farm a few miles away a spirited gray yearling was growing stronger and more powerful. My father said he could have trained himself.
Television's first equine celebrity, Native Dancer would win twenty-one of his
twenty-two races, make the cover of *Time* magazine, inspire fan mail from ma-
trons who didn't know a furlong from a furlough, and turn an already swell-
headed kid into a vicarious braggart who went around telling people he was
"Bill Winfrey's boy."

The Ponies Are Talking

BY HOLLY MENINO

A former Olympic dressage rider on the United States Equestrian Team, Lendon Gray is now a leading instructor and commentator. In this selection from *Forward Motion* by Holly Menino, we see the efforts of a dedicated and intelligent instructor in providing the framework for the education of a horse and rider (and in the process we learn a few valuable things about training).

"They have no syntax," the Stoics reasoned about animals, "therefore we may eat them." My friend Roger is less self-serving but shares this belief about animals and language. On a weekend trip to Saratoga, he went to the track but did not bet. "I'll step up to the window just as soon as the ponies start talking."

Lendon Gray knows the ponies are talking, and she knows how to talk pony. The two-time Olympic dressage rider and the people who train under her spend their days—or, at the very least, their weekday mornings—working out the syntax of classical horsemanship. This is the same horsemanship that Keith Taylor trains for in the first phase of combined training, and its movements are also the basis of a show jumper's skill. But at Lendon's Gleneden Farm, dressage is practiced intensively as a discipline unto itself.

Lendon has a big, clear voice. It is pleasant and it is very loud. She may be riding a turn at one end of the huge indoor arena and giving instructions to a pupil riding along the other end, and when her voice reaches the student on the horse, I'm sure it is still loud. It seems remarkable to me that Lendon can speak at the same time she is riding, let alone analyze someone else's riding and call out instructions to improve it. She is putting out a good deal of physical effort, and this is something many riders I've talked with feel is generally unrecognized—"Yeah, all you gotta do is sit up there, right?" was the way one of Keith's event rider friends typified the general run of ignorance among sports fans. But Lendon is able to ride, watch her students, and articulate what they should do. It is impossible to ignore, but her voice always suspects that it is being ignored. "You have asked the question," Lendon declares, "and now you must have an answer. You *must* get an answer."

Fifi Clark, like most of Lendon's clients, is female. She is tall and in her fifties, silver and gold patrician. She is fit and determined and riding a hefty bay mare. It is ten o'clock in the morning, when traffic in the Gleneden arena near Bedford, New York, is at its peak. Just north of New York City only a few miles from the Connecticut border, Bedford, the village and the outlying homes, scatters judiciously among private grassy hills, old trees, and stone walls. You can't see many of the houses from the road. Similarly, the house and barns on the farm where Gleneden is housed are set back from the road at a protective distance. Lendon's operation shares the estate with a thoroughbred breeding facility. The indoor school is the largest of a group of yellow buildings set in the middle of shady, fenced paddocks and protected from travelers on the county road by a lane with a security gate and the big maple trees that border the road. The cars parked in the stable courtyard are Mercedeses, BMWs, and Volvos. Lendon has left her much-used Subaru just beyond the wide door to the indoor arena and made a quick circuit through her office in the front of that building before heading out to the mounting block, where one of the Latino grooms waits with a small gray horse. Five other women have brought their horses into the building. There is a lot of discussion going on, many attempts to talk pony.

In its strict meaning, "dressage" is simply the training of the horse. In use, though, dressage has become the art and intensely competitive sport of training in the classical movements. Like figure skating, dressage emphasizes the power and beauty of motion, and competitors in the sport are judged on accuracy and the élan with which they perform prescribed movements. The movements the horse and rider are asked to perform depend on the horse's stage of development. At the lower levels, the tests demonstrate simple movements with long intervals of modulation between different gaits and maneuvers. The higher the test level, the more difficult the coordination asked of the horse and the more rapid the transitions between movements.

Lendon Gray is one of the most successful practitioners of dressage in the United States. She has won more national titles than any other trainer in the country, and she has become known for her ability to make brilliant, expressive horses out of unlikely candidates. She has a round valentine face and a small, sweetly shaped mouth. She is forty-six, not large, but she carries herself with the same great authority carried by her voice. Sitting a horse, she looks taller. She is straight and supple, centered, and there is relaxed symmetry in her activities. When she enters the grand prix arena in formal attire, her concentration is fierce, a force that shuts out show grounds, audience, judges, everything except the white boundary of the arena, the letters that mark the points of transition, and the responses of the horse under her. This concentration is evident in her riding at home. Somehow, although she is answering my questions and supervising the other women riding in the arena, her focus never drifts from her horse, Last Scene. A small gray horse with black legs, he has delicate, refined ears and the round dark eyes you see in illustrations of ponies in children's books. He is the horse Lendon has most recently introduced to the movements of the grand prix test, the ultimate competitive goal of a dressage horse.

Big windows above the long sides of the arena allow daylight to fall on the riders' heads and the soft brown footing. Hoofs grind the tanbark into fine shreds and mix it with the animals' manure. Most of the women here are clients. They pay Lendon to stable their horses under her management and ride under her tutelage. As is typical of dressage riders, most of these students develop an intimate knowledge of their own particular horse. While they do not actually handle routine stable work, they devote many hours beyond their time in the saddle to their horses. They become keen observers of horse motion, always on the alert for some encroachment on their horses' soundness, and they put a good deal of thought into the details of the horses' well-being, feeding and fitness, turnout and blanketing. One longtime observer of horse sports remarked to me that a dressage rider could look at the horse standing in his stall and instantly detect a new fly bite on the animal.

Although some of Lendon's students compete in dressage, a number of them ride with her for the sole purpose of initiation into the art. They are the legatees of a school of horsemanship that dates from Renaissance Italy but was first put forth humanely as a "scientific" system in 1623 by Antoine de Pluvinel, who ran a finishing school for young noblemen and was the riding instructor of Louis XIII. His *Manège du Roy,* a philosophical dialogue about the horse and its proper education, guided many other riding masters across the Continent who were entrusted with the education of aristocrats. In the manège, the riding school, the activities of the horse were routinized as gaits and movements. He was taught to travel straight forward by "treading the ring," trotting or galloping along narrow paths, and to be "just" in his turns by repetition of various exercises.

In Lendon's arena also, each woman rides a deliberate pattern. Each horse keeps his own cadence, and the arena reverberates with muffled polyrhythms cut through by the voice of Lendon Gray. She works like a ballet master with dancers as they work on their exercises at the bar—exhorting them, calling our sharp corrections, tapping a leg here, reaching up to reposition a hand. Keith Taylor has progressed through many of these lessons with Play Me Right and through the less complex tasks with Faktor. Play Me Right, for instance, can canter sideways and forward at the same time, the legs on either side of his body reaching past the legs on the opposite in the lithe X—no small feat of coordination—and Faktor does well in the turns and bends and adjustments in speed that are expected of a horse in the more elementary dressage tests. By way of becoming competitive in combined training, Keith has had to become a rider who could compete in dressage at the middle levels of the sport. The skills Play Me Right develops for the dressage phase are essential to the balance, thrust, and precise footwork the horse will call upon in the cross-country and stadium jumping phases.

What is different about the movements Last Scene performs with Lendon is the degree to which his balance is shifted back into his hindquarters. He is building tremendous isometric strength in his back end, and this allows him to be so light off his front end that Lendon can control an impressive range of motion with imperceptible movement of her seat and hands. When she gathers Last Scene back into himself like this, he is "collected," and collection is the legacy and mode of the manège. Beginning with the likes of Pluvinel and his British counterpart, the Duke of Newcastle, Renaissance trainers began to incorporate this rebalancing of the horse into a system of training that evolved in parallel with the very different techniques for educating horses and riders for military operations in which the rider leaned or perched forward on the horse. These military methods appear to have their origins among the nomadic warriors of Eastern Europe, for whom speed was a far greater consideration than poise or precision. Tension between the techniques of the manège and the traditions of the cavalry and hunt field has been ongoing. It has produced lively theoretical debates and a good deal of cross-fertilization among diverse schools of equitation, and it continues to act as a dynamic link among contemporary teachers and masters.

Dressage, the art for art's sake school of horsemanship, does not involve the speed or danger of other horse sports, but many top riders have left fast times and big fences for the intellectual stimulation of manège and the rigor of its search for purity of movement. Among Lendon's students, there are artists, cooks, lawyers, financiers, and an actor. They are, on the whole, people who understand the rewards of submitting to a discipline. As practiced at Gleneden, dressage is an ongoing process of development in which competition is an optional test of progress. It is a continuum of momentary performances as transitory as passages of music, and each of these performances is the result of the rider's intimate communication with the horse.

The big stolid bay mare carrying Fifi Clark is thundering along pleasantly. Everything about this mare is large, weighty. She is heavy equipment going to work. But there is something about the way the horse is responding that Lendon does not like, and it sends her voice up a few more decibels. "She is *ignoring* you. *Demand* an answer."

The silence Lendon hears is the curve of the mare's body as it trots a circle. She will not accept it. Although she continues to engage in dialogue with her own small gray horse, she keeps after Fifi until something shifts briefly. The change is momentary, but it is the answer Lendon was listening for.

"Good, Fifi—*super!*"

The language Lendon's students struggle with is unuttered. Its grammar is split-second sequencing of physical cues—the insistence of the legs, the tightening of fingers, the pressure of rein on bit and bit on mouth, the straightening of the rider's back, the sinking of her loins. This is the nature of riding because it is the nature of the horse. Horses do make sounds, and we have the words "neigh" and "whinny" to label them. But horse noise is usually an uncontemplated call, and what prompts it is some kind of need, such as hunger or, because horses are intensely social and their society depends on physical proximity, separation from other horses. But even when the horse is communicating with others in his herd, noise is cruder expression than what the horse achieves with his body. Dominance and fear, love and elation, are explained by one horse to others in terms of motion and place—where a horse puts her body, how he carries his tail, the curve of her neck, the angle of his ears.

Movement is the basis of our communication with horses, from trivial conversation to artistic endeavor. It conveys the subtlety of horse thought and horse intention. Lendon doesn't talk about *language*. She doesn't tell her students they are learning a language or insist they conjugate the verbs correctly as she did when she was tutoring Latin and Greek at Sweet Briar College. She assumes the language is there, and she assumes that her students are just looking for the right vocabulary. Later, when I began to visit Anne Kursinski, I found that she makes the existence of this language explicit in her teaching and writing about show jumping. Once a dressage rider herself, Anne still talks pony, and in her book on technique and training, she advises all who would ride to be aware that that is what they are doing, using language. When you sit behind the horse's shoulder and wrap your legs around his sides, you are in the conversation pit, the physical center of the animal. The sides of some horses vibrate, making a connection of your nerves with theirs. The sides or others seem dead, not like living matter but like a mattress. Either way, every impulse of the horse will pass through you, every word the horse says—if you can only hear.

Lendon listens to all kinds of horses. She is a democrat. In the dressage world, where big horses with extravagant movement have created the standard, this makes her an iconoclast. She rides some of these big horses, but just as often she rides diminutive Arabs, quarter horses, Morgans, ponies of various descriptions. She rides horses that have been schooled for the jumping arena, ex-racehorses, cutting horses, and once she brought out a horse that had been trained for the sole purpose of dog and pony shows. She believes in the process of dressage, that it will make even the most homely unaccomplished animal more beautiful and capable. In her hands, this is what happens. One of her clients has a small gray Arabian. On a summer weekend Lendon showed the horse in lower-level dressage and won the division. Two weeks later, she reported with great pride, the horse's owner, an endurance rider, won a hundred-mile competitive trail ride with him.

Under Lendon even the most ordinary animal works toward the highest levels, and she is openly sympathetic to the particular difficulties each horse must overcome. For riders, though, her patience is short. It can be stretched only by a student's absolute concentration on the work of getting the lingo down. She is kind and critical by turns as her riders adjust their posture or give up some tension Lendon identifies in a hand or an elbow. She snaps if a corner is ridden lazily in a shallow arc. She suggests, she demands, she implores so that riders working under her can do what she does on the little gray: sit their horses and understand the physical reverberations.

Lendon's gaze falls on another student, another faulty movement. This rider is a young, slight woman on a small stallion. It is a pretty bright bay and delicate enough that I had to look twice to determine its sex. The rider, who is named Karen, is sitting pretty enough, but evidently she is only passively engaged. A few minutes earlier, Karen withdrew a glove plaintively to demonstrate a callus the rein was leaving on the side of her finger. On the finger was a diamond the size of a throat lozenge. Lendon was not interested in the diamond or the callus. She was interested in how the little stallion was going and now she wants more from this rider. She criticizes the way the rider moves the horse through a corner. In a louder voice she demands a better turn. Then, forbidding another turn like the other, she places her own horse in the corner to force the line that will be ridden.

"Karen! How *can* you keep riding this way? I asked you for a *fast* trot. Do you think that's *fast?* Karen! Is he even *trotting?*"

Sweat begins to run down from the corners of Karen's eyes. Her makeup drips to the front of her T-shirt. This is not enough to bring any mercy, because Karen is making no effort to change.

"What are you thinking? I mean, *are* you thinking? Karen . . . *stop* the horse. Get off."

None of the other riders in the arena takes any notice of this. They are initiates, practicing toward the same perfection Lendon has shown them, and each of them has been caught in her sights at one time or another. They know her frustration is nothing personal. It is a question of correct movement. Lendon steps up on the little stallion and puts the question forcefully with her legs against his sides. The stallion lurches forward briefly, then recovers and gives Lendon her answer: intentional motion. He digs in and surges rhythmically along the wall of the arena.

"*This,* Karen, is *fast.*" She is talking about speed the way the jazz drummer Tony Williams talks about playing fast, rhythm that responds to a heightened accounting for the passage of time.

"See what I mean?" She dismounts and hands the reins back to her student, who avoids her gaze. "It's very clear, isn't it?"

She gets back aboard Last Scene and rides over to the observation seats and grins at me. "I couldn't let you go home without seeing me really get started." The next time I see Karen she herself will be riding Lendon's Last Scene. I think this is far too generous of Lendon, since Karen is too reticent to ride the horse as he needs to be ridden. But Lendon says it's not really so generous. Last Scene has a lot to tell Karen.

Early the first morning I visit Lendon, before the commuter traffic peaks and Lendon's clients can break free from the demands of their suburban households, the arena in Bedford is very quiet. I can hear a car go by way out on the road. I can hear the pigeons that preside from the steel rafters. Even in her absence, Lendon's voice is a presence. Her head working student, Liz Britten, is riding, and, watching her, I see the implications of Lendon's efforts with horses and students.

Like other working students, Liz is an apprentice who assumes responsibility for chores in the stable in return for Lendon's mentorship. She is very tall, a couple inches over six feet. Her dark hair is drawn away from her face in a classic chignon. She is a beautiful girl with wide-spaced eyes and lifting brows. Liz is much younger than Lendon, and patience dominates her manner—which is a good thing, since she spends a large portion of every day riding young horses, talking pony, repeating herself endlessly. But before her other riding begins, she rides Medallion, a horse Lendon has trained to the grand prix movements. There is some very fancy talk going on, an artful conversation concerning one of the most difficult movements a horse can perform, the *piaffe*. Except for the cadenced blows of the brown gelding's hoofs, the arena is silent. Liz attends to the horse, a meditative incline to her head, and Medallion attends to Liz with extreme effort. He is teaching her something.

Medallion has performed *piaffe* countless times. He knows how it goes, he knows the steps. But lifting each leg in correct sequence and cadence requires particular balance and intense coordination, and in order to accomplish these movements, Medallion needs to hear the words. They come from Liz's seat and hands, and they remind Medallion of the *piaffe*—ah, *that* move! As soon as he recognizes Liz's intention, he creates the movement. The horse draws himself together, as if he may squat down, but what he does is to remain in place, performing a slow and extravagant trot. It is heart-stopping in its intensity and exhilarating in its power.

Piaffe has been taught since the early Renaissance, but Liz could not know the movement until she had ridden it on a horse that had been schooled in *piaffe*. Medallion has the *concept* of *piaffe*. It is a horse concept, and having learned it from Lendon, he now understands the movement well enough to lead Liz to the physical instructions for it.

Medallion is now absolutely fluent in *piaffe* and the other movements that comprise the grand prix test. Lendon has spent years of physically and mentally demanding work to ratchet up the level of her communication with the horse, and most of what comes out of this work is self-awareness. Medallion is aware of his movement and his ability to assert control over it. When the horse completes a movement and can surge off into the next without correction, he assumes great authority, and when his work is over for the day, he saunters about the arena on a loose rein, his ears forward and his eyes wide. He senses his worth, and he makes it clear that the work is important to him. When it is interrupted, he feels a loss. Earlier that year, Liz had surgery on her leg. She was not able to ride but she continued in her work around the stable. Medallion began to express unhappiness. When anyone would pass his stall, he presented his face in the Dutch door and laid his ears back sourly. This brought no results, so he began hanging over the door to make sure no one would miss his glowering. Then one morning as Liz hobbled down through the shed row, he leaned far out into the aisle, caught her sleeve in his teeth, and pulled her to him. At some level he understands that he and Liz are undertaking something together. He wants to make the moves because movement is the way the horse defines himself. Prowess is his meaning.

It doesn't take much to pervert this meaning. The horse is a big, powerful, and very sensitive animal, and the use of force or even just clumsy expression can violate the horse's understanding. It's just a short trip over the boundary pointed out in a common saying quoted by Danish trainer Bengt Ljundquist: "Where art ends, violence begins," and at virtually every dressage competition where I've seen brilliant riders, I've also seen riders who cause their horses pain and confusion. They lack the physical equipment—they are too tense, they are too fat, or they ride too little—to speak the lingo. They lack the education. They jounce. Their hands jerk involuntarily at the horse's mouth. Their bodies pound the horse's back. Their legs flap at the horse's sides, their spurs digging randomly. They lack syntax. They can't talk pony.

On a cold March day I visited a stable in Connecticut where the footing outdoors was treacherous and forced the riders to crowd into the indoor arena. A woman brought a stiff black horse to the mounting block. The lady was well educated, pleasant, and in fact had a job teaching somewhere. She had just been to a dressage clinic, and the old horse was in for it. He knew it. The white of his eye showed as she climbed aboard. She put her spurs to him and worked on one rein. When he made a tentative effort, she repeated the abuse. In a minute or two the horse was hopping frantically. Even in the frigid arena, sweat broke out on his neck. She worked at him. He threatened to go up. She turned him in a dizzying little circle, a technique she had probably been shown to deal with rearing, but rearing caused by something other than herself. After fifteen minutes the old horse was in a lather and unable to trot forward, walk forward, or move naturally in any direction. The lady dismounted in frustration. "I just don't know what his problem is today." She did not know which questions to ask. She lacked syntax. She lacked even a basic vocabulary. Her old black horse was doomed to meaninglessness.

If you picture this horse and then turn to Last Scene, you will understand why dressage is a tradition of masters and students. It saves horses from bewilderment and makes brilliance possible. Lendon is part of the tradition of mastery. "I didn't choose this, you know," she has told me about riding. "I needed a job." This pragmatic explanation works, but she is too Yankee to explain also that the only reason it works is that, like Keith Taylor, she has the touch.

She grew up in Old Town, Maine, one of four children. Her father built the canoes for which the town is known, and she tells me he was also one of the first people in the country to experiment with water skis. Her mother came from a well-to-do family and brought to Old Town the first pleasure horse the local people had seen. The only people who rode there were kids who piled onto ponies, and they called Mrs. Gray's horse the "piggyback horse." The couple kept horses for the children, and Lendon and her older sister took intense and competitive interest in riding.

When Lendon went to prep school, she found she could make money by teaching people to ride. Later at Sweet Briar, she rode under Paul Cronin, who was interested in "educated" riding and had begun to systematize an approach to training hunters and jumpers based on the so-called forward seat that was becoming popular in this country. It would be several years before Lendon was introduced to the idea of collecting power and balance in the horse's hindquarters. She majored in classics, and after she graduated, she stayed on at Sweet Briar, teaching riding under Cronin and tutoring girls in Latin and Greek. During this period she became interested in event riding, and this led her to Margaret Whitehurst.

An independent and unusual person in her own right, Peggy Whitehurst had been a talented amateur rider with friends who rode on the early U.S. Olympic teams after World War II. She went on to become a commercial pilot for Pan American—evidently gender barriers had not yet been erected in the airline industry—and then married a physicist and settled on a farm in Tuscaloosa, Alabama. Using a couple of thoroughbred stallions and mares of various breeds, she began to develop a strong strain of homebreds, and by judicious pairing of these animals with top trainers, has produced horses that made the U.S. Equestrian Team lists for show jumping as well as dressage. But when Lendon came to the Whitehurst farm, her assignment was to develop the horses for combined training.

At that time, there was only nascent interest in dressage as a discipline unto itself, but when one of the Whitehurst horses, a mare named Crown Juel, began to make it clear that her talents lay outside running and jumping, Peggy said, "Why don't you try her in dressage?"

Lendon had never seen a horse perform a grand prix test and still hadn't when she took on a horse named Beppo to try for a berth on the U.S. team that would go to the 1978 World Championships. She shipped the horse to Maine for a few lessons with Michael Poulin, who coached her well enough that she was able to travel with the team to Europe as an alternate. Peggy Whitehurst continued to be a strong presence and support. Lendon took Beppo to the 1980 Alternate Games and around the same time began working with Peggy's Seldom Seen, the first horse Lendon herself trained to the grand prix level and the first of Lendon's "ponies," the small horses she has pitted successfully against the much larger, heavier types associated with dressage.

If you look at photographs of Lendon on horses during this period, you see that remarkably little has changed in the round, generous face, the small chin, the owl rims of her glasses, or the absolute correctness of her position. But details of angle and attitude show her eagerness as well as some uncertainty. How could she have known what she was in for?

At the time, Americans were even less competitive in world-class dressage than they are now. The European riders were backed by centuries of training and theory, bloodlines and study. Dressage as both an art and a competitive sport had been developed extensively—so much so that there were even styles of riding associated with particular countries. American riders had only one Olympic medal to their credit, a bronze won in 1932 by a military officer named Hiram Tuttle. Not many people in the dressage community knew enough to advise Lendon. Michael Poulin, who is known for being brilliant and quixotic, had respect for the classical principles and an intuitive understanding of what motivates a horse. He was based only an hour or so from Old Town, where she had grown up, so she didn't really have to leave home to ally herself. It was physically grueling—she was a working student and rose at three in the morning to be at Poulin's for a lesson at six before she started work—but it was productive. He gave her a lot, and even though she eventually paid off the actual bills, "I never did pay for what he gave me."

Peggy understood the obstacles that faced American riders, and although she was not able to foot the whole bill herself, she helped raise money to send Lendon to Europe to test Seldom Seen in the big time. According to Lendon, the Europeans were completely unaccustomed to seeing a little horse work in the same arena as their own breeds they had developed for the sport. But she says the European judges were more open to Seldom Seen's potential than the judges at home.

Stationed beside one of the first arenas Lendon rode into, a judge—one of three analyzing the ride—watched Seldom Seen's entrance wearily. "He probably thought, 'Oh, these damned Americans—what next?' " He lit up a cigarette and slouched down in his chair to endure the ride. As Seldom Seen was working through the first extended trot, the judge's eyes lifted. He straightened a little more when she rode into the half-passes, and by the time the little horse struck off into *passage*—which is essentially *piaffe* carried into forward movement—the cigarette was out. The skeptic was upright, dictating responsibly to his scribe.

Lendon and Seldom Seen did not take Europe by storm. She was there to watch and learn, to absorb as much of the techniques and theory that could work for the horse and her. She and Seldom Seen acquitted themselves well enough and they returned home to challenge the competition. There was a willfulness in all this, a young American on a pint-sized horse running through donated funds to ride with the elite in Europe. It was a will to know and to master. In dressage, as in art and music and literature—any endeavor where mastery is embodied and transmitted through personality—teacher-student relationships are complex.

Lendon left Poulin's operation in 1987. She was competing successfully with him, but at the same time she realized how dependent she had become on him, that she really missed having him tell her what to do in competition and even in day-to-day training. She says she is determined not to foster that kind of dependency in her own students. She wants them to exercise some initiative and try to work things out with their horses for themselves, as she does with Last Scene.

The little gray is aptly named. He is, in fact, the last of Peggy White-hurst's competition horses. When I saw him for the first time, he had been in training with Lendon for seven years, and although he was highly educated, he was just beginning to compete in the movements that Medallion knows so well. If he could sustain the physical and mental demands of high-level train-ing, he would develop even further until he too achieved mastery. Along the way, he would compete, and in spite of the hours she has invested in this horse, Lendon's ambitions for Last Scene are tempered by pragmatism. She points out that when it comes to competition, size can be a limitation. A small horse like Last Scene will have to do more—he will have to be more brilliant, and he will have to move with greater amplitude—in order to achieve the same marks as one of the big horses typical of the sport. Lendon met those challenges suc-cessfully with Seldom Seen, and it is altogether possible that Last Scene will also be able to make size irrelevant. But Lendon does not let her uncertainty about the horse's prospects in competition distract her from working toward Last Scene's eventual development. This will be a moment-by-moment pro-cess, and even as she mounts up, she is making each moment count.

When Lendon swings up on Last Scene and asks him to move off, two things are transformed, the horse and Lendon Gray. Last Scene grows rounder, like a horse in a Renaissance print, more powerful and precise in motion. He gains authority, and as I watch him change, I wonder if Last Scene's experience is something like what happened to me on a dance floor in California. There was a good orchestra, more than forty strings, playing Viennese waltzes. My partner, whom I had met moments before, was an expert on Schubert who had recently returned from a year in Vienna. I knew the box step. He could waltz. He was a strong dancer, and even in the first bars of music, I was waltzing, flying through intricate embellishments of the basic movements as if I knew what I was doing. But I couldn't have begun to replicate the steps after he released me. I don't remember his name or his face, but I remember with precision how his arms felt. His hold gave me authority, and I suspect this is what Lendon gives Last Scene.

Seated on the horse, she is elegant. She has long-legged grace, quiet poise, and when the horse is making his biggest moves, her body barely moves against him. She is carried effortlessly. When Lendon dismounts, she is an ordinary person again. She is no longer statuesque, just a woman of medium height and medium weight. She walks as if she's pushing something—a grocery cart or a stroller—and her hair bobs with every stride. When she looks away from the horses, she talks girl talk. "I *love* the sweater," she tells a client, a jewelry designer, and comments to me about her artistic verve: "Everything she does is that way. She *designed* this watch." She is often impressed by her students' accomplishments in business and art and with the horses, and her students seem to sense her appreciation of them. When they step down from their horses, they appear to leave behind any worries or resentments about the day's work. There is laughter and talk about parties and shows and shopping. The next morning, pony talk will transform them again.

When things work—when the conversation really flows and Last Scene carries Lendon through a pirouette at the canter—whose art is it anyway? *They have no syntax, therefore we may push them around?* Lendon may call the tune, but is she some kind of tough guy waggling a revolver at the feet of a victim—"Now *dance*"? The themes of this literature belong to the horse. They are natural ways of going—trotting, running, acting sexy—made self-conscious. Artifice and the motive to apply it are Lendon's contribution, but no rider could have dreamed up the movement if horses had not first shared their potential to create the movements and to take pleasure from them.

A good rider teaches this potential to her horse. A bad rider invites destruction of what comes naturally and could have been heightened by the horse's intentional participation. An indifferent rider creates a hack. A hack is oblivious to art. A hack ignores self-potential for art. What distinguishes Dorothy Parker from Eudora Welty is the difference between a hack and a horse. In much of her work, Parker, amusing as she was, took small things and made nothing of them. Welty saw the potential of small things and made magic of them.

The Riddler, my own sturdy horse with the quizzical blaze, is a hack. It isn't his fault. He is a good enough horse with a good enough heart, but he is ignorant. He talks only pidgin pony, and this is the fault of a series of indifferent riders, the last of them me. My ignorance compounds his. Out on the trail, we move together well. But on these outings we don't talk much. Things are fine until, like the woman trying to ride the old black horse, what I have in mind is beautiful. I ask him to move forward and sideways at the same time, but Riddler's answer is to lift his head and quicken his strides. I ask again. The jaw stiffens, the legs move faster. I squeeze harder with my legs. It is only when he begins to struggle with his head that I finally get the message and relax my grip on the reins. The horse lowers his head and goes ahead, traveling just slightly sideways.

The Riddler may be more prone to misunderstanding than a young horse in a good school. He is older, with memories of humans that cause intense anxiety, and when he is visited by one of these memories, he stops in his tracks and shakes and sweats. Since he doesn't talk good pony, he has only limited forms for expressing these memories and creating happy ones. But a rider like Lendon Gray could expand his expressive range and his trust.

I wish I could—and so do thousands of other people in this country, or at least the thirty thousand members of the U.S. Dressage Federation. It's a pastoral yearning, like the ones that send people out of the city to places populated by other creatures of different minds. People want to howl with the wolf. They want to fly with the condor, swim with the dolphin. They want to ride the horse. But with horses our relationships have become a culture by now, so you can't just buy your ticket and hire a guide. You have to learn the lingo.

Perhaps it is the limitations of so many riders that have brought psychics into vogue with horse owners. For a fee, they will speak the horse's mind to its human. Lendon reported with wonder and wry humor the experience of one of her clients. His game old horse was showing considerable stiffness at the beginning of each ride, but he would go on with his work until the gimpiness disappeared. His owner dialed a psychic in California, and the medium gave a rather lengthy report of what was on the horse's mind. This included two pertinent statements: "I like being part of things even though my feet hurt. I need salt." Almost any aging horse still in work could have made the first statement, but the complaint about the salt applied specifically. When the owner checked the horse's stall, he found that out of thirty-some salt holders in the stable, only his horse's was empty. The experience rattled Lendon enough to make her reluctant to consult a psychic. "I might be horrified by what some of these horses would say about me."

What the horse says *to* her, however, is urgently important. Pony talk may be the language of patience, but it is also the source of Lendon Gray's impatience. She is aware of an imperative need to get the lingo down quickly. A move made wrong is a scale with a wrong note that once played will take hundreds of other performances to make the phrase right and beautiful. She remains keenly aware of the risk of failing with a particular horse, of failing to ride, and this is what makes her raise her voice at a student. "Now. Do it *now.* Please. . . ." The fact that a student is well known or dauntingly wealthy or powerful will not make Lendon back down or even tone down. "I'm getting old . . . *now!*" Dressage is long. Life just may be enough time.

Personals

BY MELISSA PIERSON

T o say that Melissa Holbrook Pierson's *Dark Horses and Black Beauties* draws from sociology, psychology and cultural anthropology would make the book seem far more academic than it is. It's not at all, as shown by this chapter, chosen for its depiction of the dynamics not only between people and horses but among the denizens of a working stable.

Yesterday I moved a ton of manure. Actually, it was the horses who moved it; I merely pitched it into a wheelbarrow and rumbled it over the rocky dirt and up to the top of the pile of more manure, then upended it and began again—a true Sisyphean task, because the cart always rolls back down, and you always have to go up once more. It gave me new appreciation for the digestive systems of these animals, with their constant need for grass or grass substitutes to be moving through the colon.

I have become one of the small army of part-time workers at Dominique's barn offsetting the cost of lessons by doing the endless things that need doing. And, indeed, she runs her establishment with martial precision, though there is never the sense that these are the kind of orders one chafes under, the kind meant to bat you into line. You just do them, because you are getting something better than money in return: the opportunity to take her orders in the ring.

We are, in fact, a small army composed of slave masters who are in turn enslaved by our slaves. We are the ones who assiduously pick up their excrement behind them, the ones who put our hands under their penile sheaths on a regular basis to make sure they're clean. We bathe, curry, brush, mane-pull, tail-detangle, hoof-pick, daub with salve, apply spray, and take off and put on blankets, fly sheets, leg wraps, bell boots. They stand there and loudly demand their food.

Yet, go into a stall; close the door. Wait a moment. Something will occur to you, something that seems to shift in the air between the two of you. It is the weight of power, the weightlessness of vulnerability, exchanging ions. The horse is there looking at you with eyes the color of chocolate pudding. He cannot escape you, or whatever it is you mean to do with him.

This particular army is rather haphazard in organization, yet everything gets done: I have never been in a stable so clean. *Standards*—the highest of them. Aisles swept, stalls picked out several times a day, water buckets scrubbed and refilled. Brushes cleaned, tack soaped. No aesthetic overlay, however: no flowers by the driveway or sign to announce the place's name, a couch barely fit for the Salvation Army in the viewing room, and, more often than not, no paper towels in the bathroom. But the working bolts, in their well-oiled condition, are their own visual pleasure. The horses, the order, the order.

The first of the two sergeants in the line of command is Amelia, barn manager. A flow of wavy light brown hair, pleasant steady demeanor, quiet. She has, Dominique says, one of the great posts—elegant, natural. This is no doubt aided by her body, which is trim and athletic and without any folderol at all. She does everything as Dominique decrees, often as she pauses in the middle of the arena while seated atop her horse: "Amelia, please give Deedee an extra flake of hay, then bring in Jesse from outside. When you're finished with that, get Dandy ready for the lesson. You can use the Wintec. Oh, and since we don't have any clean pads, look through the pile to find the best—I think Wilant's will be okay; he didn't exactly sweat today." Stuart, the second sergeant, is a friendly ex-city refugee with buzz-cut red hair, a former teacher of guitar. He likes to have music on as he works, Lou Reed or occasionally *Classical Music's Great Waltzes.* On it goes: "Stuart, you can do the buckets on this side, and then a quick pick run on the other." Along with the stacking of hay and shoveling of sawdust, Stuart builds and fixes everything from new paddocks to tack boxes to a hayloft and additional stalls.

Then there is Catherine, Dominique's protégée. She's like any pretty teenager with porcelain skin and fine lemon-colored hair; her cheeks flush deep rose as she spends hours picking rocks out of the paddocks under a hot summer sun at Dominique's request, but it seems she doesn't sweat. She has one of those purely American, corn-fed, "large-boned" frames, completely in accord with that of her seventeen-hand horse, Fury, whom she rides in dressage competition. She wants to go as far as she can, she says, to Grand Prix if possible, "though most people don't know just how much work this is." She has the legs to be able to communicate with the big ("Yeah, a big teddy bear!") animal. Another frequenter of the barn comments with a laugh how butch she looks when riding with two whips: "Pop-pop-pop! Man, I love it!" Catherine and Dominique are more like school pals than teacher and student separated by more than twenty years; they crack up uncontrollably when one of them says, "People hear the name *Fury* and expect this great wild thing—ha ha ha!"

Besides Stuart and one other fellow who has come in for a lesson or two, everyone who works there or learns there is female. (Dominique jokes that she is going to rename the place Tits-in-Front Farm, since that is the posture correction she makes most constantly.) That is, until Dominique advertises in *The Chronicle of the Horse* for a full-time working student and gets Frank.

I talk with him as I stand in the tack room oiling Dominique's double bridle, so new it is stiff and the black dye comes off with the saddle soap. I ask him where he comes from; I am curious ever since two days ago, when I first saw him momentarily doff his ever-present cap to reveal his balding head and suddenly appear much older than I thought he was. His lanky body, perfect for the old-fashioned thigh-balloon breeches he favors, makes him look exactly like one of those young British cavalry officers of the twenties or thirties who used themselves to illustrate their own riding manuals. Now I realize: *Not just starting out—starting over.*

He has previously worked with standardbreds, raising and training harness racers. Now, he says, the stakes are getting too rich for his blood, with good yearlings going for fifty thousand dollars and Canadians and even Europeans getting involved more and more. He moved to another stable nearby, but some family intrigue or other—he was very vague—made him want to leave.

He says he is here now, beginning a new thing entirely, because he is motivated to become a better horseman. Because all of the good horsemen he knows are good people, too. There is a correlation at the deepest level, he says: compassion for the animal, desire to do right, the need for "clean living." I sense he is not referring to lots of carrot juice and regular visits to the gym; this is the old construct, and I smell religion lurking nearby, just as I feel sadness coming off him even when he means to reveal nothing.

I watch Dominique as I do my work, and I get good at not gawking too obviously. She reminds me of a dog trainer I knew, a trainer whom people accused of committing miracles. There is that look of tight focus, the tendency to teach by praise, and to come down on a fault "like a bolt of lightning," in the trainer's words, and just as quickly to release the pressure. When a couple of horses in the box stalls that line the two aisles are participating in some foolishness together—"They want attention," she says, "but I'm going to show them that's not the way to get it"—her body suddenly compresses, losing a fifth of its size. She moves so fast it's as if she's done a sci-fi teleportation, suddenly disappearing from the arena only to reappear near the tack room, where she picks up a dressage whip. In another flash she's in Wilant's stall. "Do you see this whip? Do you see that wall? I am hitting that wall"—*whap, whap, whap*—"so you know never, never to do that. And you, too"—now she's in the next stall—"don't play around with"—*whap*—"that crap. I've had it." She closes the door and walks away. The horses have not been frightened, exactly; they look like students who have been caught out. A few minutes later she looks back at Wilant, who now bears a different look, and she interprets it in cartoon-character words: " 'What'd *I* do? *I* didn't do nothin'!' " She laughs.

Then she is schooling a student's horse, and she talks incessantly. "*Good* boy, *good* boy—whoops, not that—I said *not* that—you're not going to do that—*good* boy—yes, yes." Of course, her body is doing the real talking. She is keeping him "round," "soft," "moving out," "gathered up," keeping him from swinging his hindquarters around as they circle, and especially from dropping his head and shoulder down as they circle to the right. Later she explains, "His head is, what—two hundred pounds? I'm not going to *carry* it for him." They canter in tiny circles, and the pace never varies.

It enlivens my time, not to mention me, to have a special horse to love. But it would be too heartbreaking, like choosing another woman's man, to settle on one of the boarders' horses; instead I choose, or am chosen by, Wilant, one of the two school horses. He is a large Dutch warmblood with a black mane and tail; a wash of dapples over his body is so light that it requires the sun to become visible. One of his eyelids droops away from his eyeball at the bottom, as if it had gotten hooked on something once.

Actually, I have fallen for him slowly, during which time he gradually became "my boy." There is something adolescent and unprotected about him. Dominique says he came from a rider who did not know how to ride him—she was not malicious, but her inabilities allowed twists and constrictions to cramp him into unhappiness. It has taken Dominique time to free him again, to show him how to flex and stretch and cure himself. He will never, though, stop hanging his great pink tongue out the side of his mouth as he works, or become angry enough for fits of head-tossing if a rider has heavy hands. While I am on his back I try to will my weight away from him so as not to hurt him; his head remains perfectly still with me because I attempt no contact at all—

a petty form of abuse, Dominique informs me, since it leaves a horse direction-less. But she is amused by the deal we seem to have struck: I won't ask him to work very hard, and he won't put up a fuss with me.

So it is a real surprise one weekend when Monica, the wealthy girl-friend of the man who financed the barn and known by some as the Con-tessa—she of the Cinderella's sister demeanor, perennially cross and critical—while showing me how to polo wrap Wil's legs (condescendingly): "Now, if you expect to do dressage, you have to learn to polo wrap"), stops and rests her hand on his rump. Her eyes squeeze into a terse black line. "If you ride him badly, I'll *kill* you."

Later Frank is working in Wil's stall as I slip in to give him a good-bye carrot; I have become a walking cliché. "You know, I have to tell you," I say, "I've sort of fallen for Wil."

"What is it about Wil?" he asks. "Everyone here's in love with him—you, Dominique, Monica."

"It's that combination of 'Please be kind, please' with this big hunk of manliness," I explain. "You know, the paradox of *Take care of me—I can take care of myself?*"

"No," Frank says.

I watch unseen from across the barn as Amelia, untacking Lupe, plants a little kiss on his withers minutes after he has bucked his way around the ring with her onboard. He is a particularly difficult case, coming from the racetrack, where the grooms liked to play a little "game" with him, turning him into a cantankerous biter. But any horse's misbehavior or difficulty seems to make Amelia soften all the more, and the louder they get, the calmer she gets. She is constantly talking to and smoothing them, even when she is talking to some-one else, unlike so many riders who seem barely to notice there's a breathing thing on the other end of the lead they're hauling on. She is becoming my model for how to be with horses, for nothing they do seems to inspire either anger or fear in her. The next horse she rides, Chocolate, has decided no one should mount him unaided from the ground, and when she tries he succeeds in tipping her over onto her rear and then runs around the ring loose. She springs up and runs toward him, waving her arms, to spook him away from the open door. Then she asks for a leg up and mounts him. She speaks in low tones to him, and he soon lowers his head in relaxation.

Frank doesn't last long; perhaps his desire for clean living is not being met here, or perhaps he does not believe that horses are as Dominique says they are, as she acts they are with every move in her repertoire. The next working student, and the ones after her, will be young women.

Likewise, Wilant does not remain alone in my affections, not after the arrival of Dutchess, a draft cross with the coloring of a cow and a head about the same size. I start loving her the moment Dominique comments that we look good together as we go around the ring—this is yet another shameful thing that speaks unkindly of my character—and I continue loving her as I build fantasies that maybe she, finally, after all these years, would be my first horse, responding to the propitious omen of my having bought a house located between those of two women who own horses. Only there is no one who will give me the twenty-five hundred dollars she will cost as well as the indeterminate amount more it would take to keep her.

She is strangely aloof, taking carrots but never presuming thereafter that they are her due. I have always been attracted to the thick exterior, and I set about trying to see if in her case it conceals a wounded softness within. I think we look for mirrors in our love. One night I dream that she has reared up to put her front legs around my shoulders in a hug, but when I wake I realize I must have conflated her with my black-and-white girl dog, who can actually do that without killing me in order to express her regard.

I sit on the floor of her stall, writing. I note that if the pen slips, it is because she is looking for, though not demanding, more carrots. Her head is down in my lap—a *big* head. Her lips are pink, wrinkled, and hairless, human skin, baby skin. I pay no attention to the music Stuart is playing—his taste describes everything mine is not, and sometimes Catherine and I exchange a glance when he leaves the barn and move as one to change the tape—but suddenly I become aware of the words Rod Stewart is singing at that moment: "You're in my heart, you're in my soul . . ." I laugh, because you couldn't put something like that in a movie; stupidly, ludicrously, obvious. Her ears are large and bovine, and her lips and tongue, though so large as well, are delicate enough to take a fingernail-size piece of the dried mango I am eating. She stands quietly over me right now, larger than life.

Good Horse Keeping

BY PAUL ZARZYSKI

P aul Zarzyski has been an amateur and then a professional rodeo bare-
back bronc rider for more than a dozen years and a writer of poetry and
prose for twice that length of time. A celebrated "cowboy poet," he has
toured the world reading his works, of which he has published several
collections.

That this entertaining and insightful selection contains the extra added
attraction of poetry makes it all the more irresistible.

Life is a catch pen full of rodeo broncs, and way I figure it, forty-six
years into this buck-out, the mission is to decide, early on, *Did you come to hide
or did you come to ride?* If the latter, it doesn't take too many seasons forked to
this buckin' horse orb named Earth before we learn the crude rude truth of
the old adage: *Never a pony couldn't be rode, never a cowboy couldn't be throwed.* And
subordinating this proverb is yet another cowpoke dictum: *Get pitched off, climb
right back on.* Rodeo, like Poetry, can get into your hemoglobin, into the deep
helices of DNA, and once there, it becomes your metaphorical makeup for life.

In Spanish, *rodear* means "to surround"; in colloquial Mexican, it means
"a cattle roundup." *A-horseback* is understood, and understood so emphatically,
that only bull riders (I can *cow*-poke fun at them here because most can't read
anyway) might disagree that rodeo *means* horses. Moreover, I think rodeo cowboys relate to horses in ways that very well could qualify them as the staunchest
of animal rights advocates. But let's put the raucous Yosemite Sam WHOA! on
opening that Pandora's Saddlebag right now and lope off instead toward a few
poems that have graced my Lariati-Literati Life because I choose to believe, my
Muse has some Annie Oakley, Mr. Ed, Saint Francis of Assisi, Midnight, and My
Friend Flicka in her bloodlines.

In the days when rodeo fever popped the cork and geysered the mercury out of my genuine Hopalong Cassidy bucking bronco thermometer, all I thought about was horses, Horses, HORSES! My focus burned so intensely that I became unable to discern the word *house* in print, which made for some interesting magazines at the newsstand. You had your *Horse Beautiful,* your *Good Horse Keeping,* your *Horse and Garden.* Same syndrome occurred with the word radio: National Public Rodeo, Rodeo Free Europe, Rodeo City Music Hall, and that little kid's wagon called a Rodeo Flyer. In any case, I'd be driving all night between rodeos and listening to the rodeo—I mean radio—to stay awake, and I'd look up at that full moon, and its Rorschach test shadow always appeared to me as the image of a bronc rider sittin' pretty in his leather throne on a high-rollin' bucker. Years later, I wrote this "rodeo romance."

THE BUCKING HORSE MOON

A kiss for luck, then we'd let 'er buck—
I'd spur electric on adrenaline and lust.
   She'd figure-8 those barrels
on her Crimson Missile sorrel—
   we'd make the night air swirl with hair and dust.

At some sagebrushed wayside, 3 A.M.,
we'd water, grain, and ground-tie Missile.
   Zip our sleeping bags together,
make love in any weather,
   amid the cactus, rattlers, and thistle.

Seems the moon was always full for us—
it's high-diving shadow kicking hard.
   We'd play kid games on the big night sky,
she'd say "that bronco's Blue-Tail Fly,
   and ain't that ol' J. T. spurrin' off its stars?"

We knew sweet youth's no easy keeper.
It's spent like winnings, all too soon.
   So we'd revel every minute
in the music of our Buick
   running smooth, two rodeoin' lovers
cruising to another—

beneath Montana's blue roan
bucking horse moon.

The Augusta show at 2, we'd place again,
then sneak off to our secret Dearborn River spot.
We'd take some chips and beer and cheese,
skinny-dip, dry off in the breeze,
build a fire, fry the trout we caught.

Down moonlit gravel back to blacktop,
she'd laugh and kill those beams for fun.
That old wagon road was ours to own—
30 shows since I'd been thrown
and 87 barrels since she'd tipped one.

We knew that youth won't keep for rainy days.
It burns and turns to ash too soon.
So we'd revel every minute
in the music of our Buick
running smooth, two rodeoin' lovers
cruising to another—
beneath Montana's blue roan
bucking horse moon.

Ahhh, "sweet youth"—and no, it's truly not an "easy keeper" (said of a horse who winters well, holding his weight on minimal feed). And though the equine species, from sixty-million-year-old eohippus (the prehistoric "dawn horse," no bigger than a cocker spaniel) to today's mustangs, has drunk out of a lot more watering holes than we Homo sapiens, they haven't discovered the fountain of youth, either. Depending on vocation, a horse is usually considered to have reached retirement age of anywhere from six to eight years (race-horses) to twelve to fourteen years (roping, reining, show horses) to eighteen to twenty-two years (ranch/stock horses). On the average, horses age approximately three years for every human year. By the time they're twenty or twenty-two, they're often referred to as "pensioners" and put out to pasture just like us two-legged folks. If there *were* an Adam and Eve, and if they *were* responsible (having bitten into that measly McIntosh) for the injustices and disparities of today's world, I especially hold against them the so-called fact of life wherein the most common four-legged members of our families—dogs, cats, horses, rabbits, etc.—enjoy only a fraction of our longevity. It ain't my fault; I don't even like apples that much, and usually wind up feeding them out of the fruit bowl to our twenty-three-year-old mare, Cody (her favorite treat, next to getting into the bird feeder). Therefore should I ever be designated Creator for a Day, one of my first duties will be to see to it that horses live as long as parrots or turtles.

Speaking of religion, of the miracle of life, of that glowing, glowering coal of youth that stays a-smolder and waiting, in most of us I hope, for a stiff wind to blow away the soot and ash and expose the fire, I watched Big George Foreman—who trained like a Clydesdale as he harnessed himself to a jeep and pulled it around his neighborhood—convincingly win a fight recently against a very strong thirty-two-year-old opponent. George is forty-eight. At the Red Lodge Rodeo years ago, I saw a black mare named High Prairie buck off the World Champion Saddle Bronc Rider and do a little soft shoe in the middle of him to add just a skosh of injury to the incredible insult. In the midst of a couple dozen cowboys straining to restrain their chuckles in back of the bucking chutes, I swear I heard old High Prairie nickering all the way back to the catchpen: ". . . never a cowboy couldn't be throwed, be throwed, be throwed." I *know* Sonny and Pat Linger, High Prairie's guardians, heard her because they made no effort at all to curb their knee-slappin' delight. By the way, that horse was thirty-three years old at the time. I wonder if Big George will still be climbing into the ring at ninety-nine?

I wish my saddle horse Buck (short for Buckskin, actually), could have lived into his George Years (Foreman, Burns) as High Prairie lived so vibrantly into hers. The morning I found him dead in the corral, I phoned the neighbor—hoping to borrow his tractor—and when, in relating my situation, I choked up and broke down, he responded, "It's just a horse." Understand that he's not a cruel man; unlike myself, who didn't begin hanging around horses day-to-day, until my twenties, he'd likely been aboard them since he was three or four; his family had owned dozens, bought and sold them, watched them come and go, live and die. Although I had come to know "intimately" hundreds of rodeo broncs, Buck was sort of my first, shall we say, partner. I don't know if my good friend and neighbor ever sat in front of the TV at midnight while eating a bowl of Wheaties, mid-January Montana windchill temps pushing eighty below zero, and thought to himself, "Wonder if my horse is craving a late-night snack, too," then bundled up in umpteen layers and plodded, like a moon-walking astronaut, to serve up a half canful of grain and a couple alfalfa flakes? Maybe he has. And maybe he's missed his lost horses as much as I've missed mine and grieved every bit as hard.

BUCK

The December my horse died, I did not
go to midnight mass
to celebrate with a single-sip of wine
Christ's birth. Instead, lit
between a nimbus moon and new snow,
I guzzled mescal and mimicked the caroling
coyotes down the crick
where weeks earlier I dragged Buck
behind the pickup—horizontal
hooves at an awkward trot
in the side mirror, an image
I'll take with me to hell. No backhoe,
no D-8 Cat to dig a grave with, I left
nim in deep bunchgrasss, saffron
Belly toward the south
like a warm porch light thrown
suddenly over those singing
No-el, No-el . . .

   "Riding the same ground
that past spring for horned cow skulls
to adorn our gates, I spotted four
bleached white as puffballs,
methodically stuffed them
into a *never-tear* trash bag,
balanced the booty
off one thigh and tried to hold
jog-trot Buck to a walk,
my forefinger hefting
the left rein to curb
his starboard glance.

One by one,
like spook-show aliens hatching
from human brisket, white shoots popped
through that hot black plastic
gleaming in moon sun that turned
my grasp to butterfat. And when I reached,
lifting to retwist my grip,
it was sputnik flying low, it was
Satan's own crustacean unleashed, it was the
prehistoric, eight-horned, horse-eating bug
that caught Buck's eye
the instant his lit fuse hit powder. Lord,
how that old fat pony, living
up to his name one last time,
flashed his navel at angels,
rattled and rolled my skulls like dice,
and left me on all fours
as he did on that Christmas—high-
lonesomed, hurt, and howling
not only holy word toward the bones.

I never again road east—toward Buck's bones. By now, I suppose someone could have picked up his skull and hung it on their gate or barn. I guess that thought bothers this former grave-robber a bit. Most ranches have established boneyards to which winter-killed stock is dragged for decades and decades. Renowned western writer Teresa Jordan offers a passage in *Riding the White Horse Home* about the critical moment in which a horseman works a colt toward the bones. The idea is to slowly and gently expose the young animal to everything and anything that might later, under sudden first-time encounters, instinctively cause him to spook. Whether they recognize it as such or not, horses do not like the look, or smell, of death. Ol' Buck illustrated this to me in no uncertain terms. I suppose most herbivores feel the same way.

The spring following Buck's departure, our mare, Cody, foaled on Memorial Day. I was in my rodeo-old forties—my riggin'-riding days pretty much history—and was struggling with resigning myself to a life between youth and death, complete with the reentry of the words *house* and *radio* into my old geezer language. I was missing then, and likely will forever miss, the challenge of, and the elation after, making a classy ride on a snappy bronc. I was also missing my rodeo *compadres*; the majority of them had, years back, begun to take on normal lives—marriages, mortgages, steady jobs, children—but the truth be known, I missed those bucking horses most, their personalities and temperaments far more akin to my own than that of fellow humans with whom I cross trails these days.

One of the premier horse gentlers in the West, Randy Rieman, who I have the honor of calling friend, is riding colts full-time for the Parker Ranch in Hawaii. He encounters very few horses that he can't coach toward feeling safe, at ease, and maybe even "fulfilled" with saddle and cowboy aboard. Randy told me recently, however, of one three-year-old, after days and days of groundwork, that bucked, under his first saddling, from 5 P.M. till sundown. A horse like that will probably wind up in a rodeo string and have a good long careeer of eight-second workdays, according to Randy. "My kind of guy," I thought, and kept the notion to myself, knowing how important it is to Randy to find—to watch and listen and feel for—whatever unique equine code and/or communication will convince each individual horse to place his trust in the funny-lookin' critter standing upright.

So Cody game birth to a healthy filly we named Rosebud—not Rodeo Rose or Widow Maker, Whiplash or Reller's Wreck, Snake Eyes, Aces-'n'-Eights, Sky Lab, Booger Red, Crash, Moonshine, or Midnight. And although it *was* Memorial Day, I felt no cemetery visitation obligation: Ol' Buck had not received a formal burial or headstone. Few horses do. One of the greatest rodeo champions of all time, however, not only has a marble, but one engraved with verse. I stood before his final resting place recently at The National Cowboy Hal of Fame in Oklahoma City and felt something powerful in both the place and the words—

> Underneath this sod lies a great
>   bucking hoss
> There were lived a cowboy he
>   couldn't toss
> His bane was Midnight, his coat
>   black as coal
> If there's a horse heaven, please, God,
>   rest his soul.

—and what I felt somehow reflected off the poem I wrote that Memorial Day in praise to parturition, equine-style:

I AM NOT A COWBOY

because cowboys don't cry and I can't fight back
my 4-H'er greenborn rapture
while watching Cody foal—no white socks up front,
a blazed face breaking through the giant dew–
drop into the 10:15 A.M. sun,
two hind socks stretched side-by-side in the dirt
like reverse white-on-black exclamation marks, and
yup *it's a filly!* Because *real* cowboys frown
unless it's a *horse colt* with four black feet,
this poem, I suppose, should tone down
its jubilation. Sorry fellers, for losing it,
but this cute little filly finds her footing
fast as you can think that single big syllable
HEART. And she stays up, pivoting
off mom's legs, like a ring-wise prize
fighter using the corner posts and ropes,
to gather herself after taking
birth's hard shot. It's Memorial Day
but these tears are not for the fallen
because I'm out here cheering on new life,
no taps bugled sat in the breeze
through these balm-of-Gileads
as the suckling foal's curled upper lip
blossoms, her gums
the pink-red rosebud-persimmon
color I think of when I think of the living,
when I think, again, of HEART. Let's rhyme it,
for tradition's sake, with *smart.*
Let's make this poem *cowboy* and make up some
for the poet, who tries but just can't quite
swallow hard enough his joy
as four more quarter horse quarter note
hooves step their first

Rosebud-with-Cody
Sorrel stroll around our corral.
                                                                        —*For Elizabeth*

Cody and Rosebud now make up one half of our quarter-horse quartet, which we consider the most interesting, in many ways, two thirds of our family of six. When we left the large ranch where Buck died and Rosebud was born, we had a hard time finding an affordable place with enough acreage on which to keep our four horse people. Folk close to our predicament admonished, "Why not sell them?" To which we sometimes replied, "For the same reasons, we suppose, you haven't opted as yet to sell Jimmy or Suzy." In my opinion there are few differences. Sure, it costs a little more to keep our horses in shoes and food, and their schooling doesn't come cheap, either—not to even mention vet bills and worming medicine. On the other hand, we didn't have to invest a single frustrating in day in potty training. There is, however, one extremely significant and difficult difference: unlike guardians of sons and daughters, we've had to come to accept, and even hope, that our horses will die before us. Only then can we ensure that their entire lives are lived with the most humane care a "people person" can offer a "horse person." On second thought, maybe God—Her Pegasus Paint Self—got it right after all?

Two Sisters

ELLIE PHAYER AS TOLD TO GERALDINE MELLON

I had the pleasure of knowing Ellie Phayer through two equestrian tourism junkets that she organized, one to Wales and the other to England's Dartmoor region. Her untimely death six years ago deprived the world of her energetic and caring spirit. This story here shows how beautifully horses can literally and metaphorically come to represent important segments of a human life.

I have a horse in Ireland. Truly, she's my horse. I've not bought her, but we all know she's my horse. Sister is a 16.3-hand dark bay. I don't know if she's the most beautiful horse in the world. I do know that never have I had such telepathy with a horse. When I'm mounted, boundaries dissolve. Horse and rider—sisters, if you will—share one body, one mind and yes, one soul.

Sister and I met one misty Irish morning on the Connemara coast, a day nearing the end of one of the legendary Willie Leahy's cross-country rides. The previous evening a fellow rider had challenged me to a race, come dawn. "A race it is in the morning then," agreed Willie. That night, without my knowing, Willie sent 90 kilometers to his stable for my special mount.

"You'll have Sister," he said next morning, and Sister stepped out of the horse box into my life. Surprised, delighted, I quickly saddled and mounted, eager for the prerace warm-up. Willie, in the meantime, set off inspecting a mile and a half of beach to make sure the "track" was safe.

From the beginning, Sister and I were of one mind. During the warm-up we connived, Sister and I. Sensing her power, I held her sharply in check. She immediately agreed with this strategy and obligingly relaxed, craftily hiding her true feelings and capabilities. Like two skilled poker players lurking behind a calm, almost lazy facade, we knew . . . we knew.

Warm-up over, Willie yet a distant pinpoint, we quietly watched the 20-odd riders stationing themselves along the course in gentle surf. Unexpectedly, my life began to flash before me. What a long way from the intellectual little Brooklyn girl, the girl whose musical talent led her to the brink of the concert stage. The young wife, mother and scholar turning to music of another sort, the lyrical magic of English and Irish literature. The young woman whose life lost its melody with the death of a beloved four-year-old daughter. Divorce. Teaching and single-parenting a son. Nervous years cured with self-doubt, grief, unnamed fear. And the son, nearly a man, gone to college.

Abruptly my thoughts returned to the race, and I gleefully anticipated flying with Sister, my Pegasus. Instantly catching the mood, she tensed, pricked ears in readiness. Not yet, Sister, not yet.

Retreating into the past, I recalled a certain horse ride, one of my first. The horse sped away at what I took for a dead gallop. Far from being frightened, I loved it and experienced total, absolute glee, the same emotion now dancing invisible pathways between Sister and me.

The "dead gallop" in my fortieth year pivoted my life, changing it forever. At age 41, alone, my uneasy world badly needing direction, I began riding. By the third lesson, I was jumping. I was making mistakes, but riding came naturally to me. From the time I started horse riding, free-floating nervousness plagued me no more. It simply disappeared. Riding competence sparked internal confidence, and fears receded into memory. Had it been eight years since my first lesson? Eight years leading me to the back of this gallant mare?

Sister stirred gently beneath me, nudging my thoughts toward the impending race. Still Willie had not returned from reconnoitering, and thoughts drifted again.

One year's riding, and I'm planning English riding holidays for college students, demanding—and getting, if you can believe it—the best riding instructors in England. By my second year, I knew I was great. That is no longer true, but in those days, I absolutely knew I was great. That second year, bent on impressing Maj. J.M.B. Birtwistle, trainer of English Olympians, I prepared to go over an indoor course of seven jumps.

"Ellie, the horse you're on stops at the fourth jump," warned an instructor.

"Not with me, he won't!" But, alas, the horse refused, while I, staying on course, cleared the jump with ease. Remounted, reluctant horse and red-faced rider cleared the jump in unison.

But something was wrong. Parts of that undergarment peculiar to women dangled near my wrists. What could I do? Heading for the next jump, I desperately tried to wiggle the offending garment into place.

"The hands," commented Maj. Birtwistle, "are very busy."

My antics undoubtedly fueled the cheeky American stereotype. Sister, I'm glad you didn't know me then.

Eight years in the saddle over hundreds of English and Irish miles and I became a weaver of dreams. My livelihood was accompanying riders to the British Isles. And to this windswept beach.

Today, Sister, the gods have blessed us, have granted us power to race the very wind. Confidence born of other lifetimes connects us. One in body, mind and spirit, we are invincible.

Suddenly, I understood that, as surely as we two were sisters and the race was ours, just as surely my life was mine, not to be lost to invading cancer. Weakened from chemotherapy, weary at the prospect of imminent surgery, I had arrived for this Connemara trek.

Willie, with uncanny Irish inkling, sensed the importance of this race, suspected the supernatural bond that would unite horse and rider. He felt it, and sent for Sister. Now joy coursed through my veins as her great body anticipated my thoughts.

The bets were in place, the markers laid, the spectators waiting, mounted in the shallow surf boundary. It was time. I licked salt spray from my lips, and we were off. I never felt her hooves cut into the sand; we were winged sisters racing our brother wind. It was no contest. The contender lagged 20 lengths when we flew across the finish line. We did it, Sister, we did it!

Later, I basked in adulation. Teenage girls braided my hair; fellow rides praised my skill. The race netted me 50 pounds, and Willie grinned, a knowing twinkle in his eye.

Still, the 50 pounds were a bit of an embarrassment. I had, after all, brought these riders to Ireland on holiday. Sister, the next day, continuing to read my thoughts, came up with the perfect solution. As we walked through a gap in a farmer's wall, a dry stone wall hundreds of years old, she cleverly arranged for me to bump my toe on a particular stone—the keystone of 14 feet of wall. Amid 30 stomping, wild-eyed, spooking horses, the wall, like so many dominoes, fell. When the dust settled, I handed my 50 pounds to the farmer.

And so the trek ended. I returned home and regained my health, as I knew I would. Two years have passed. We two remain sisters of spirit, often sharing misty green miles. Ireland shines as my special joy.

I have a horse in Ireland.

Permissions Acknowledgments

Bill Barich, "Dreaming" from *The Sporting Life*. Copyright © 1999 by Bill Barich. Reproduced with the permission of The Lyons Press.

Stephen Budiansky, "Tallyho and Tribulation" from *The Atlantic Monthly* (September 2000). Copyright © 2000 by Stephen Budiansky. Reprinted with the permission of the author.

Esther Forbes, "Breakneck Hill" from *Grinnell Review*. Copyright 1944 by Esther Forbes. Reprinted with the permission of Frances Collin Literary Agency.

Dick Francis, "A Royal Rip-Off at Kingdom Hill" from *Classic* (June/July 1976). Copyright © 1975 by Dick Francis. Reprinted with the permission of Sterling Lord Literistic, Inc.

Gilbert Frankau, "Mustard-Pot, Matchmaker" from *Men, Maids and Mustard-Pot* (New York: The Century Company, 1924). Copyright 1924 by Gilbert Frankau. Reprinted with the permission of Timothy d'Arch Smith.

Ben K. Green, "Sleeping Sickness" from *The Village Horse Doctor: West of the Pecos*. Copyright © 1971 by Ben K. Green, renewed 1999 by Jaime C. Taylor and Martha K. Taylor. Reprinted with the permission of Alfred A. Knopf, a division of Random House, Inc.

James Herriot, Chapter 19 from *All Things Bright and Beautiful*. Copyright © 1973, 1974 by James Herriot. Reprinted with the permission of St. Martin's Press, LLC and David Higham Associates, Ltd.

Nancy Jaffer, "Nona Garson" [editor's title, originally titled "Riding High on the Grand Prix Circuit"] from the New Jersey *Star-Ledger* (May 26, 1997). Copyright © 1997 by The Star-Ledger. Reprinted with permission. All rights reserved.

Maxine Kumin, "Why Is It That Girls Love Horses?" from *Ms.* (April 1983). Copyright © 1983 by Maxine Kumin. Reprinted with the permission of the author.

Ring Lardner, "Tips on Horses" from *The Ring Lardner Reader,* edited by Maxwell Geisman. Copyright © 1963 by Charles Scribner's Sons, renewed 1991 by Ring Lardner, Jr. Reprinted with the permission of Scribner, a division of Simon & Schuster, Inc.

Beryl Markham, "Was There a Horse with Wings?" from *West with the Night.* Copyright 1942, 1983 by Beryl Markham. Reprinted with the permission of North Point Press, a division of Farrar, Straus & Giroux, LLC., Laurence Pollinger, Ltd. and the Estate of Beryl Markham.

Cookie McClung, "From Sailboats to Snaffles in One Easy Marriage" from *Horsefolk Are Different: A Selection of Short Stories on Horse Experiences.* Copyright © 1987 by The Chronicle of the Horse, Inc. Reprinted with the permission of The Chronicle of the Horse, Inc.

Thomas McGuane, "Buster" from *Some Horses.* Copyright 1999 by Thomas McGuane. Reprinted with the permission of The Lyons Press.

Holly Menino, "The Ponies Are Talking" from *Forward Motion.* Copyright © 1996 by Holly Menino. Reproduced with the permission of The Lyons Press.

William Nack, "Pure Heart" from *Sports Illustrated* (1990). Copyright © 1990. Reprinted with the permission of the publishers. All rights reserved.

Ellie Phayer as told to Geraldine Mellon, "Two Sisters" from *Straight from the Heart,* compiled by the editors of *Equus.* Copyright © 1997 by Fleet Street Publishing Company. Reprinted with the permission of the Primedia Equine Group.

Melissa Holbrook Pierson, "Personals" from *Dark Horses and Black Beauties.* Copyright © 2000 by Melissa Holbrook Pierson. Reprinted with the permission of W. W. Norton & Company, Inc. and Granta Books.

Alois Podhajsky, "School Horses, the Most Important Assistants of the Instructor" from *My Horses, My Teachers* (New York: Doubleday, 1968). Copyright ©

1968 by Alois Podhajsky. Reprinted with the permission of Trafalgar Square Publishing and Buchberlage Ullstein Langen Muller.

Damon Runyon, "All Horse Players Die Broke" from *Guys and Dolls: The Stories of Damon Runyon*. Copyright © 1992 by Sheldon Abend. Reprinted with the permission of Viking Penguin, a division of Penguin Putnam Inc. and Penguin Books, Ltd.

Andy Russell, excerpt from "Horses and Horsemen" from *Trails of a Wilderness Wanderer*. Copyright 1970, 1988 by Andy Russell. Reprinted with the permission of The Lyons Press.

Felix Salten, "The Imperial Spanish Riding School" from *Florian, the Emperor's Stallion* (Indianapolis, Ind.: The Bobbs–Merrill Company, 1934). Copyright 1934 by Felix Salten. Reprinted with the permission of Sanford J. Greenburger Associates.

Jane Smiley, "Mr. T's Heart" from *Practical Horseman* (October 1999). Copyright © 1999 by Jane Smiley/Horse Heaven. Reprinted with the permission of the Aaron M. Priest Literary Agency, Inc.

Gene Smith, Chapter 10 from *The Champion*. Copyright © 1987 by Gene Smith. Reprinted with the permission of Scribner, a division Simon & Schuster, Inc. and Curtis Brown, Ltd.

Red Smith, "A Vote for Ta Wee" from *The Red Smith Reader*, edited by Dave Anderson. Copyright © 1970 by Red Smith. Reprinted with the permission of Phyllis W. Smith.

William Steinkraus, "On Winning" from *Reflections on Riding and Jumping*. Copyright © 1997 by William Steinkraus. Reprinted with the permission of Trafalgar Square Publishing.

Paul Trachtman, "The Horse Whisperer" from *Smithsonian* (May 1998). Copyright © 1998 by Paul Trachtman. Reprinted with the permission of the author.

Carey Winfrey, excerpt from "Tip on a Lost Race." Copyright © 1972 by Carey Winfrey. Reprinted with the permission of the author.